KOBE

I remember when, as a kid, I got my first real basketball.

I loved the feel of it in my hands.
I was so enamored with the ball
that I didn't want to ruin the pebbled leather grains
or the perfect grooves.

— Kobe Bryant, *The Mamba Mentality*, 2018

Mamba Forever:

Kobe Bryant's
Life & Legacy
In His Own Words

CONTENTS

3. Quotes about Kobe Bryant

Chapter 1

INTRODUCTION

A shocked and grief-stricken world population, upon learning of the death of Kobe Bryant, his daughter, and seven others in a helicopter crash, immediately turned to the World Wide Web to post photos to share their loss: a moment in time when people came together to mourn. But of all the photos that appeared online, in newspapers, magazines and on television, one image stands out—it was a center punch to the heart.

It was posted on the day they lost their lives in a sudden, unexpected crash in Calabasas, California on Sunday, January 26, 2020. The tweet was posted at 7:34 p.m. on Twitter by @_nightingaleee, captioned: "The kids who were waiting for Kobe and Gigi in Mamba Academy." It had an emoticon of a broken heart, hashtagged #RIPKobe #RIPGianna.

That sports facility in Thousand Oaks, owned by Kobe, was filled with adults but mostly children who were awaiting his arrival for a basketball game, subsequently canceled.

The stricken look on the faces of the children breaks your heart. On their knees, gathered in small groups, some of them holding basketballs with their heads down, they had gotten a stark reminder that life—in all its beauty, in all its joy—is counterbalanced by pain and sorrow, light and darkness. It's an image that will stay with me forever.

The worldwide media coverage accorded to Kobe rivaled that of John Lennon, whose tragic death was also sudden and unexpected. But in both of their cases, what they had to say about life, about how to *live* life, not for oneself but for others by paying it forward, is the best there is in humanity.

Retiring from the Los Angeles Lakers after the 2015-2016 season, Kobe Bryant, a man of wealth and means, could have retreated from public view to become a recluse, to enjoy retirement in whatever way he wished. He could have done that, but he didn't. That wasn't Kobe's way. Instead, he used his celebrity and wealth to pay it forward, repaying the debt he owed to those who came before him. They helped him learn how to become one of the best basketball players in the world, and how to realize his potential, personal and professional.

Was Kobe perfect? No, but who among us are? He was mortal, subject to human failings, but we remember him for his triumphs, not his transgressions. He threw himself into coaching children, knowing that the discipline required to learn and master basketball, no matter what one's life goals are, would serve in good stead, laying a firm foundation for a happy, productive life.

Kobe also began a second career as a storyteller, starting a company using sports as the nucleus for stories that would inspire children and young adults, lift their spirits, and show them how wondrous, how beautiful, and how meaningful life can be. Life, as he reminds us, is not about fame or money or any of the other ephemeral things that distract us from its real purpose—to live a productive, meaningful life by living for others, to celebrate life and all it has to offer.

It is that spirit of life that defined Kobe Bryant, and that is why he will be remembered for a very long time.

Chapter 2

KOBE BRYANT ON HIMSELF

Much has been, and will be, written about Kobe Bryant, but the quotations in this section, drawn from 20 years of his career, lets us understand how he felt, in a way that interpretive texts, analyses, and speculations cannot: we get Kobe's voice, straight from the heart. We "hear" him speak for himself.

Note: textual comments in italics are by the editor/writer.

Aging

You get older. You start seeing the beauty that's in that process. You start trying to find love in that, find the beauty in that, which is completely different than being 21. (bleacherreport.com, interviewed by Bleacher reporter Kevin Ding. ESPN.com, quoted by Joseph Zucker, "Kobe Bryant The Interview: Key Takeaways, Comments from NBA TV Special," February 16, 2015.)

Aloofness

The aloofness thing, honestly, I didn't really hear about it until later. A lot of it was just naive, because I didn't read the papers. I didn't watch the news. I had no clue what was going on, what people were saying about me. It sounds silly to say, but it's true. And I think because of that, a lot of people looked at it like, "*Woah*, he must be arrogant." But I didn't know what the hell was going on. I had a reporter one day come up to me and ask me about it ... "think you're arrogant, what's up with that?" And it absolutely just seemed to come out of left field. I was just like, "What are you talking about?" And he was like, "Haven't you read the papers?" From that day forward, I started reading the papers. (esquire.com, Mike Sager, "Kobe Bryant Doesn't Want Your Love," November 2007.)

Analyzing basketball games

I felt like it's important for the next generation to learn how to watch film, how to study the game. I felt like if this show was around when I was 10 years old, 11 years old, I would have gained so much insight, so much value from it, that by the time I'm 22, 25, my knowledge of the game would be at a much higher level than my predecessors. I feel like it's part of my responsibility to give back to the next generation, try to share and teach some of the things I have learned from some of the great players, great mentors, great coaches that I've had. *His insights appear on ABC, and sports channel ESPN+.* (theundefeated.com, Kelley D. Evans, "Kobe Bryant is gearing up for the 2018 NBA playoffs," April 12, 2018.)

A new challenge

It's fun to figure out the journey, but it's also extremely frustrating. Things don't move as fast you want them to. But that's OK. *Re: Kobe Bryant as the principal in his own multimedia company, Granity Studios.* (*USA Today*, Mark Medina, "Life after basketball: Kobe Bryant's transition to Oscar, Emmy winner and AAU coach," January 23, 2020.)

Attending Lakers games after retirement

I have a life and I have my routine at home. It's not that I don't want to go [to Lakers games], but I'd rather be giving B.B. [Bianca Bella] a shower and sing Barney songs to her. I played 20 years and I missed those moments before. For me to make the trip up to Staples Center, that means I'm missing an opportunity to spend another night with my kids when I know how fast it goes. ... I want to make sure the days that I'm away from them are days that I absolutely have to be. I'd rather be with them than doing anything else. (latimes.com, Arash Markazi, columnist, "Column: Kobe Bryant won't be at the Lakers' opener—he has a more important game to attend," October 21, 2019.)

Basketball camp at 15 years old

At this basketball camp, back in the States, I was...120 pounds, soaking wet. I'm standing with my dad and the scouts knew him. And one tells my dad there's a kid here who's supposed to be really, really good, the No. 1 player in the world. His name is Kobe. And my dad says: "That's my son!" And the scout grabs my arm and says, "You don't look like no No. 1 player." (nytimes.com, Philip Galanes, "For Arianna Huffington and Kobe Bryant: First, Success. Then Sleep," September 26, 2014.)

Being himself

I do all of life's daily tasks. The other day my wife and I stopped at 7-Eleven and I pulled up to the pump and I started to pump some gas. She went inside to buy something and was waiting in line. The guy in front of her sees me outside but doesn't see her. He says, "Man, there's Kobe Bryant pumping his own gas." My wife says to the guy,

"He wipes his own ass, too." She came back out and we had a big laugh about it. We both have the same sense of humor when it comes to stuff like that. But, yeah, I do the same things as everything else. (espn.com, uncredited, "Kobe Bryant talks MJ, LeBron & *Django*, undated.)

Being liked

Some people are going to like me, some people aren't going to like me. The people who don't ... just have to understand who I truly am, and that can only happen through time. That's why you don't see me doing talk shows and things like that." (SI.com, "Kobe Bryant, Through the Years," SI.com Staff, January 26, 2020.)

Be yourself—not like Mike

I don't want to be the next Michael Jordan, I want to be Kobe Bryant. (bet.com, Paul Meara quoting a tweet from Mateo Estrada, January 26, 2020.)

Black mamba

I had to organize things. So I created the "Black Mamba." So [I] has to deal with these issues, all the personal challenges. The Black Mamba steps on the court and does what he does. I'm destroying everybody that steps on the court. (usatoday.com, Steve Gardner, "Six Kobe Bryant quotes that define NBA legend's career," January 26, 2020.)

Breaking up the Bulls

The city of L.A. knows *me* now, and they know who I am. But at the time, the perception was that Kobe was trying to break up the team. That was wrong. I am a maniacal worker, and if you're not working as hard as I am, I am going to let you know about it. That's why Shaq and I still have a good relationship: He knows I have zero fear of him. I would tell him what he was doing and what he wasn't doing. And vice versa." (gq.com, Chuck Klosterman, "Kobe Bryant Will Always Be an All-Star of Talking," February 18, 2015.)

Caron Butler

He's dealt with real pressure. He's dealt with life-altering situations. So when he steps on the court, nothing fazes him. To tell a teammate that he's not working hard, to challenge people at practice is nothing to Caron. He's challenged people who were carrying weapons. ... Hopefully kids will read it and see something in it for their own journey. No two journeys are the same, although the emotional challenges each person faces are very similar. But they can see how he handled his challenges and perhaps find courage and bravery in their own dark moments. (Foreword by Kobe Bryant in *Tuff Juice: My Journey from the Streets to the NBA*, by Caron Butler, 2016.)

Changing careers

Twenty years is a long time [to be a NBA ballplayer]. The challenge also has to shift to doing something that a majority of people think us athletes can't do, which is retire and be great at something else. (*New Yorker*, 2014, quoted in the Los Angeles Times, Obituary, "Kobe Bryant Dies in crash," January 27, 2020.)

Cheetah inspiration

When you watch me shoot my fadeaway jumper, you'll notice my leg is always extended. I had problems making that shot in the past. It's tough. So one day I'm watching the Discovery Channel and see a cheetah hunting. When the cheetah runs, its tail always gives it balance, even if it's cutting a sharp angle. And that's when I was like: My leg could be the tail, right? ... Inspiration surrounds us. (nytimes.com, Philip Galanes, "For Arianna Huffington and Kobe Bryant: First, Success. Then Sleep," September 26, 2014.)

Chicago Bulls: Michael Jordan

His technique was flawless. I wanted to make sure my technique was just as flawless. (Twitter, Mark Medina (@ MarkG_Medina), February 16, 2015.)

Coaching

Coaching youth sports is so important to take very seriously because you're helping the emotional [development] of young kids. So it's understanding not to be overcritical and understanding that (there) are going to be mistakes (*USA Today*, Mark Medina, "Life after basketball: Kobe Bryant's transition to Oscar, Emmy winner and AAU coach," January 23, 2020.)

Comeback attempt

I want to see if I can. I don't know if I can. I want to find out. I want to see. What I'm going to do is do what I always do: I'm going to break everything down to its smallest form, smallest detail, and go after it day by day. Just one day at a time. (bleacherreport.com, Joseph Zucker, "Kobe Bryant The Interview: Key Takeaways, Comments from NBA TV Special," February 16, 2015.)

Competitiveness

That's a big misconception of my competitiveness. People look at my competitive spirit, and they automatically attach it to the thing that's most similar, most easily recognizable, which is Michael Jordan's competitive spirit. I'm different. I enjoy building. I enjoy the process of putting the puzzle together, and then the byproduct of that, the consequence of that, is beating somebody. That becomes the cherry on top, the icing on the cake. But the thing that's most enjoyable to me is not actually beating you. It's the process of coming up with the blueprint of beating you that I enjoy. That's a huge flip, so for me I enjoy building. I enjoy coming up. So the transition for me is a little different than it is for other guys. (usatoday.com, Sam Amick, "Kobe Bryant Q&A: Future, fashion, legacy and Lamar Odom," February 26, 2015.)

Compulsion

You can't stop an artist from painting a picture. You can't slow him down. (bet.com, Paul Meara quoting Kobe, interviewed by Bonnie Bernstein, January 26, 2020.)

Daughters

And lastly, our daughters, Natalia, Gianna and Bianka... you guys know that if you do the work, you work hard enough, your dreams come true. You know that. We all know that, but hopefully, what you get from tonight is the understanding that those times when you get up early and you work hard, those times when you stay up late and you work hard, those times when you don't feel like working, you're too tired, you don't want to push yourself, but you do it anyway—that is actually the dream. That's the dream. It's not the destination, it's the journey. And if you guys [can't] understand that, then what you'll see is you won't accomplish your dreams. Your dreams won't come true. Something greater will, and if you guys can understand that, then I'm doing my job as a father. (etonline.com, Emily Krauser, "Kobe Bryant's Family Joins Him for Numbers Retirement Ceremony With the Los Angeles Lakers," December 18, 2017.)

Demise

It's a comfortable one. It's an understanding that you can't have life without death, can't have light without the dark, right? So it's an acceptance of that. When it came time to decide whether or not to retire, that's really an acceptance of that mortality that all athletes face. And if you combat it, you'll always have that inner struggle within yourself, you know what I mean. (The Ringer, video interview on YouTube.com, "Death, Mythology, and Basketball: An Interview with Kobe Bryant," November 10, 2016, quoted in people.com, "Kobe Bryant Opened Up About Mortality in 2016 Interview: 'Can't Have Life Without Death,'" January 27, 2020.)

Desire

From the beginning, I wanted to be the best. I had a constant craving, a yearning, to improve and be the best. I never needed any external forces to motivate me. (*The Mamba Mentality: How I Play*, by Kobe Bryant, 2018.)

Dreams

Just keep your dreams alive, don't let anybody tell you what you can and cannot accomplish. (ksdk.com, Ashley

Cole, Rene Knott, "Kobe Bryant's advice to Knott's son in 1998." January 27, 2020.)

Early years in Italy

I was lucky to grow up in Italy. I was taught extreme fundamentals: footwork, how to create space, how to handle the ball, how to protect the ball, how to shoot the ball. I wasn't the strongest kid at that camp. I wasn't the fastest. I wasn't the most athletic. (*Sports Illustrated*, 2013, quoted in the *Wall Street Journal*, Ben Cohen, Joshua Robinson, Rachel Bachman, "Lakers Legend Won Five Titles," January 27, 2020.)

Ego

I'm not interested in self-serving pieces. It has to be something where an athlete reads it and is inspired by something, learns something and pushes themselves. ... I enjoy passing things on. Some people want to take it with them to the grave. Like *Lord of the Rings*. The world is filled with a lot of Smeagols [who] can't let go of the damn ring. (espn.com, Ramona Shelburne, "Kobe Bryant never stopped trying to inspire," January 27, 2020.)

End of a basketball era

I can't say it is the end. I thought the Spurs were done 20 years ago. Those guys are still winning. So, to answer the question, I can't say this is the end of my era because I thought their [era] was done and they're still there. So I'm hoping I can have the same rebirth. (ESPN.com, quoted by Joseph Zucker, "Kobe Bryant The Interview: Key Takeaways, Comments from NBA TV Special," February 16, 2015.)

Enough is enough

My heart can take the pounding. My mind can handle the grind. But my body knows it's time to say goodbye. And that's OK. I'm ready to let you go. I want you to know now. So we both can savor every moment we have left together. The good and the bad. We have given each other all that we have." (nbclosangeles.com, Associated Press, "Kobe Bryant Announces Retirement in Letter Penned 'Dear Basketball,'" November 29, 2015.)

Favorite teacher

She was so good and so passionate about what she was teaching about writing and storytelling. She firmly believed that storytelling could change the world. And she opened my eyes to this passion I didn't know existed. (The *New York Times*, Sarah Mervosh, "A Lasting Friendship: Kobe Bryant and His High School English Teacher," January 28, 2020.)

Fear of failure

Unfortunately and fortunately [I] fail quite a bit but I understand that is actually part of the process of succeeding. I'm not one that really believes in failure. I believe that you have setbacks. You have to learn from those. You have to learn what are those landmines that can be avoided the next time, what are those pitfalls. You have to learn from that stuff. You have to welcome those things. It's a part of life. (glassdoor.com, Amy Elisa Jackson, "Game Changer: Can Kobe Bryant Dominate Off the Court?", November 2, 2016.)

Focusing on surgery

Reality gives nothing back and nor should you. Time to move on and focus on doing everything in your power to prepare for surgery, ask all the questions to be sure you understand fully the procedure so that you may visualize it in your subconscious while being operated on and better the chances of its success. Then focus on the recovery process day by day by day. It's a long journey but if you focus on the mini milestones along the way you will find beauty in the struggle of doing simple things that prior to this injury were taken for granted. This will also mean that when you return you will have a new perspective. You will be so appreciative of being able to stand, walk, [and] run that you will train harder than you ever have. You see the belief within you grow with each mini milestone and you will come back a better player for it. (businessinsider.com, Scott Davis, "11 of Kobe Bryant's most inspirational quotes," January 26, 2020.)

Forever a student

You guys know what a student I am of the game. I know every series that the Lakers have played in. I was just a Laker nut, and I know every Celtics series, I know every statistic. (The *Orange County Register*, Kevin Ding, "Kobe Bryant's post-Game 7 interview," June 17, 2010.)

Friendship with Michael Jordan

(*When asked if Jordan was a mentor and an influence.*) Still is to this day, we are still extremely close. He told me, "If you ever need anything, just call me." And we've been close ever since. (sikids.com, "What It's Like to Interview Kobe Bryant," Isabel Gomez, April 14, 2016.)

Gaming and competition

I'm a competitive individual, so if there's a competition involved, I'm all for it. I came from an extremely competitive household, and games between me and my cousins would get ruthless. Everything in my family was about bragging rights, so if you could beat someone using the worst team in the game, that was the best. It was all about challenges. (ign.com, "Kobe Bryant Interview," undated.)

Gianna shattering a stereotype

Dude, man, I'm telling you—the best thing that happens is when we go out and fans will come up to me and she'll be standing next to me and they'll be like, "Hey, you got to have a boy. You and V[anessa] got to have a boy and have somebody carry on the tradition, the legacy. She's like, "Oy, I got this. You don't need a boy for that." I'm like, "That's right. ... You got this." (The *Hollywood Reporter*, Evan Real, "Watch Kobe Bryant Praise Daughter Gianna, an Aspiring Basketball Star, in 2018 Interview [Jimmy Kimmel]," January 26, 2020.)

Gianna handling the pressure of a game-winning shot

She looks up, looks at it, she closes her eyes, and takes a couple of deep breaths. She completely calms down, and she goes to the free throw line, and drains them. Wins the game. Alright man! (Fox 11: Los Angeles, Kelli Johnson, "Kobe Bryant talks about his daughter Gianna handling the pressure at the free-throw line," in an interview with Liza Habib, January 26, 2020).

Gianna's middle school basketball team

It's been fun! We've been working together for a year

and a half and they've improved tremendously in that time. I've got a group of great parents, a group of really intelligent, hardworking girls, and—they're all seventh graders, they're all 12 years old—but they've been playing so well! I play 'em up now. They've been playing eighth and ninth grade, they've been winning tournaments. But the most important thing is they keep improving, keep getting better and they love doing it. They love being around each other. (etonline.com, Desiree Murphy, "Kobe Bryant Filed 'Mambacita' Trademark for Daughter Gianna Less Than a Month Before Their Deaths," January 27, 2020, quoting from a December 2018 interview by her.)

Giving his all

I'm thankful. I'm not sad at all. I left no stone unturned. I gave everything to the game for 20 years in the NBA and more before that. So I feel very thankful to be able to play this game this long. (usatoday.com, Martin Rogers, "The Kobe Bryant interview: 'I'm not sad at all,'" April 27, 2016.)

Greatest of all time (G.O.A.T.)

(*When asked what Shaq would be like if he had Kobe's work ethic.*) He'd be the greatest of all time, for sure. He'd be the first to tell you that. I mean this guy was a force like I have never seen. I mean, it was crazy. ... A guy at that size... Generally guys at that size are a little timid and they don't want to be tall. They don't want to be big. Man, this dude was...he did not care. He was mean. He was nasty. He was competitive. He was vindictive. (deseret.com, Herb Scribner, "Kobe Bryant says he and Shaq could have won 12 rings. That's right, 12," August 28, 2019.)

Helicopters

But then traffic started getting really, really bad and I was sitting in traffic and wound up missing things like the school play. I had to figure out a way I could still train and focus on the craft [of basketball], but also not compromise family time. That's when I started looking into helicopters to get up and back [from training]. *Note: For obvious reasons, Kobe and his wife agreed that they'd never fly on the same helicopter.* (nzherald.co.nz, uncredited, "Kobe Bryant detailed decision to start flying in helicopters in heartbreaking interview," January 28, 2020.)

High idle

Last year was the best basketball I've played in my entire career. I've never worked so hard in my life to prepare for a game, in film study, quarterbacking on the floor, putting everybody in the right position, and then having to take care of my body. It was literally no life, because my body was hurting so much. I had to ice-bath, stretch, massage, elevate my legs, stretch, and then go out and play. But the results were irrefutable. It doesn't stop. It becomes life, you know? To be at that level, that's what you have to do. (The *New Yorker*, Ben McGrath, "The Fourth Quarter," March 24, 2014.)

Hiring women

We just find the best for the job. I never really bothered to ask them how they felt about taking this job in the first place. It never even dawned on me to ask it, like—listen, we've all done our homework; we've all done our research.(*Commenting that at Kobe Inc., 71% are women:* Washingtonpost.com, Kent Babb, "The Revisionist," November 14, 2018.)

Homework

I want to learn how to become the best basketball player in the world. And if I'm going to learn that, I gotta learn from the best. Kids go to school to be doctors or lawyers ... and that's where they study. My place to study is from the best. (businessinsider.com, quoting Showtime's "Muse," Scott Davis, January 26, 2020.)

Inspiration

The most important thing is to try and inspire people so they can be great in whatever they want to do. (bet.com, Paul Meara quoting a tweet by Tony Dombrowski, January 26, 2020.)

Inspiring the next generation

Playing basketball, the focus is always winning. Winning championships. Winning championships come and go. It's going to be another team that wins another championship, another player that wins another MVP award. If you really want to create something that lasts generations, you have to help inspire the next generation, right? They create something great. And then that generation will inspire the one behind them. That's when you create something forever. And that's what's most beautiful. (businessinsider.com, Eugene Kim and Connor Perrett, "Kobe Bryant once said that he wanted to be remembered as an investor instead of an athlete," January 26, 2020.)

Intensity on winning playoffs

The urgency is there just because it's there. ... To me it's about winning another one, just because I want to win another one. (The *New York Times*, Jonathan Abrams, "An

Intense Kobe Bryant Is Acting Grumpy," June 9, 2009.)

Investing in children's futures

They're our future. It's important to invest in them. They have dreams, they have ambitions of being a future MLS star. It's important we invest in them and educate them. (abc7.com, ABC7 Eyewitness News, posting on Twitter, January 26, 2020.)

Kobe on his coach Phil Jackson

So part of that was him trying to tame me. He's also very intelligent, and he understood the dynamic he had to deal with between me and Shaq. So he would take shots at me in the press, and I understood he was doing that in order to ingratiate himself to Shaq. And since I *knew* what he was doing, I felt like that was an insult to my intelligence. I mean, I knew what he was doing. Why not just come to me and tell me that? ... I was finally like . . . I'm done with this guy. I'll play for him and win championships, but I will have no interaction with him." (gq.com, Chuck Klosterman, February 18, 2015, "Kobe Bryant Will Always Be an All-Star of Talking.")

Leadership

If you are going to be a leader, you are not going to please everybody, you have to hold people accountable. (silverscreenandroll.com, @LakersSBN, February 16, 2015.)

Learning from Obama

In sports, you get better by working in the gym. I wanted to know how he got better, from managing his schedule to what he reads. And because he gets sports, and we can talk about that, too, it makes it easier to have that connection. (On a trip to the White House to see then-President Obama. politico.com, Ben Strauss, "What Kobe Bryant Misses Most About Obama," June 6, 2017.)

Legacy, Personal

At the end of my career I want people to think of me as a talented overachiever. I was blest with talent, but I worked as if I had none. (foxwilmington.com, Gregg Re, "Kobe Bryant: Jim Gray recalls NBA star's final interview in uniform," January 27, 2020.)

LA Lakers franchise

The thing about this franchise is that you shouldn't need recruiting to come here. It takes a special person to want to play for this franchise and take the pressure that comes along with playing for this franchise. The pressure of following Magic's [Johnson] footsteps, and myself, and the dynasty that we've had. It takes a special person to do that. If I need to convince you to come here to carry that legacy forward, you ain't the one to be here. (slamonline.com, Ryne Nelson, "Kobe Bryant Says Lakers 'Shouldn't Need Recruiting' for Free Agents to Come," February 16, 2018.)

LA Lakers legacy

I want to say, thank you so much for tonight. But it's not about my jerseys that are hanging up there for me. It's about the jerseys that were hanging up there before. Without them, I couldn't be there today. They inspired me to play the game at a high level: Magic [Johnson], Cap [Kareem Abdul-Jabbar], Shaq [Shaquille O'Neal] pushing me every day, [Elgin] Baylor. [Walt] Chamberlain. [Gail] Goodrich. [Jerry] West. [James] Worthy. It goes on and on. And secondly, it's about this class organization...and it's also about the next generation, this current Lakers roster that we have here. It's about embodying the spirit that exists in those jerseys up there and carrying this organization forward so that the next 20 years are better than the past 20 years. That's what it's about. (*At Kobe Bryant's retirement ceremony at Staples Center.* etonline.com, "Kobe Bryant's Family Joins Him for Numbers Retirement Ceremony With the Los Angeles Lakers," December 18, 2017.)

Mamba mentality

Having infinite curiosity in what you do. Constantly asking questions. Why is that that way? Why is that here? Why is that there? That'll lead you down the rabbit hole of answers that lead to more questions, and that's how you get better at your craft. At its purest form it's curiosity and learning on top of that. (reddit.com, photographer Andrew D. Bernstein interview with Kobe Bryant, date unknown.)

Making sacrifices

We all can be masters at our craft, but you have to make a choice. What I mean by that is, there are inherent sacrifices that come along with that. Family time, hanging out with friends, being a great friend, being a great son, nephew, whatever the case may be. There are sacrifices that come along with making that decision. (CBS Sports 2014 Documentary, "Kobe Bryant's Muse," quoted by Hannah Frishberg, "Kobe Bryant's best quotes about life," January 27, 2020.)

Marriage

Commitment and [the] competitiveness of "We're going to succeed." That's all the beauty of it: having the persistence and determination to work through things—very, very tough things—and we've been able to do that. (All the Smoke Full Podcast, Matt Barnes and Stephen Jackson, Episode 11, January 8, 2020.)

Michael Jordan

When I have the chance to guard Michael Jordan, I want to guard him. I want him. It's the ultimate challenge. (usatoday.com, Steve Gardner, "Six Kobe Bryant quotes that define NBA legend's career," January 26, 2020.)

Mindset

I never looked at [basketball] as work. I didn't realize it was work until my first year in the NBA. When I came around, I was surrounded by other professionals and I thought basketball was going to be everything to them and it wasn't. And I was like, "This is different." I thought everybody was so obsessive about the game like me. It was like, no? Oh, that's hard work. I get it now. (ESPN, quoted in businessinsider.com, Scott Davis, January 26, 2020.)

Missing the media limelight

Am I going to miss any of this? Probably. Maybe. Yeah. I've done a lot of interviews here standing in front of this locker and the one that I'll always remember is the night I ruptured my Achilles. Yeah, I'll miss standing here and watching you [media] elbow each other [for position] and all that fun stuff." (*After his last postgame interview.* Espn. com, Baxter Holmes, ESPN Senior Writer, "Kobe Bryant gives his last locker-front interview, March 28, 2016.")

Most direct route

"I've decided to skip college and take my talent to the NBA." (*This prompted Jon Jennings, director of basketball development for the Boston Celtics, to remark, "Kevin Garnett [21 seasons in the NBA, for the Timberwolves, Celtics, and Nets] was the best high school player I ever saw, and I wouldn't have advised him to jump to the NBA. And Kobe is no Kevin Garnett."* (SI.com, "Kobe Bryant, Through the Years," SI.com Staff, January 26, 2020)

NBA wake-up call

When I first came into the NBA, I was one of the first to come out of high school. I was seventeen years old—at the time the NBA was much more grown-up. It wasn't like now. I thought that you come into the NBA, you play basketball all day. The thing I was most excited about was coming to the NBA not having to worry about writing a paper or doing homework. It was basketball all day, this is awesome. (esquire.com, Mike Sager, "Kobe Bryant Doesn't Want Your Love," November 2007.)

Next Michael Jordan

When you're looking at players out there now, you're saying, "OK, there's *not* a next Michael Jordan." It's not about the surface stuff. It's about: Are they approaching the game the way he did? ... *That* is what it means to be a Michael Jordan—to be a Kobe. *That* is what we should be looking for. (bleacherreport.com, Howard Beck, "The Ghost of the Goat [Greatest of All Time]: Why There Isn't A 'Next Michael Jordan' Anymore," April 26, 2017.)

No fear

I wasn't scared of missing, looking bad, or being embarrassed. That's because I always kept the end result, the long game, in my mind. I always focused on the fact that I had to try something to get it, and once I got it, I'd have another tool in my arsenal. If the price was a lot of work and a few missed shots, I was OK with that. (*The Mamba Mentality: How I Play*, by Kobe Bryant.)

No pain, no gain

I just love to play. I just kept trying to figure out different ways to play through things and you know it was basic logic to me if there was any reason the injury wouldn't get worse, I'm going to play through it. If it's an injury that's just painful and I can navigate the pain then I will be fine, I will play. But I didn't play with things that would lead to career ending things. (usatoday.com, Martin Rogers, "The Kobe Bryant interview: 'I'm not sad at all," April 12, 2016.)

Not missing basketball

It's crazy! Honestly, I don't miss it. Basketball's not who I am, it was what I did but it doesn't define who I am. That's just part of the challenge for me now, to be able to move on from basketball and successfully do other things. (complex.com, Twitter: @TefTobz., "Interview: Kobe Bryant on What's Next, Mamba Mentality and His New Collection with Nike," November 1, 2017.)

Oscar win for "Best Animated Short" for *Dear Basketball* (90th Academy Awards)

At the 90th Academy Awards, in Hollywood. I've always been told that as basketball players the expectation is that you play. This is all you know. This is all you do. Don't think about handling finances. Don't think about going into business. Don't think that you want to be a writer—that's cute. I got that a lot. What do you want to do when you retire? "Well, I want to be a storyteller." That's cute. This is ... a form of validation for people to look and say, "OK, he really can do something other than dribble and shoot.'" (Theundefeated.com, Kelly L. Carter, Kobe Bryant: "Oscar nomination is proof I can do 'something other than dribble and shoot," March 3, 2018.)

Outsider

It was different. I didn't understand the slang, I was a little Italian boy, I didn't understand the fashion ... and I couldn't spell, so the teacher told my mother that I was probably dyslexic. It was like somebody took me and dropped me in a bucket ... in a tub of ice cold water, because it shocked the shit out of me. ... No matter what happened in life I could step on the basketball court and let my game speak to that. And that feeling of playing with that rage was new to me. (theatlantic.com, Terrance F. Ross, "Kobe Bryant's *Muse*: A Carefully Candid Look at an NBA Legend," February 28, 2015.)

Pain and tolerance after injury, and coming back

There are certain things that my body can't do that I used to be able to do. And you have to be able to deal with those. First you have to be able to figure out what those are. Last year when I came back, I was trying to figure out what changed. And that's a very hard conversation to have. So when I hear the pundits and people talk, saying, "Well, he won't be what he was." Know what? You're right! I won't be. But just because something evolves, it doesn't make it any less better than it was before." (si.com, 'Twilight the Saga," Chris Ballard, not dated.)

Parents

My parents are my backbone. Still are. They're the only group that will support you if you score zero or you score 40. (goalcast.com, Flavia Medrut, "25 Kobe Bryant Quotes to Help You Overcome Every Challenge," December 28, 2018.)

Passages

It's simple. I adjust to the reality of the situation. Accept it. Be aware of the rage and accept it while focusing on having the mind for this challenge which entails patience, teaching and understanding. Different challenges call for different approaches. This isn't a death to me so much as it is an evolution, a transformation, or as Joseph Campbell would say, "the new normal." (*On moving on in life.* espn.com, spoken to Ramona Shelburne, February 6, 2016, quoted in "Kobe Bryant never stopped trying to inspire," January 27, 2020.)

Perspective

When I was a rookie in my first training camp in Hawaii, I ordered a bowl of cereal from room service. They were Frosted Flakes with a little thing of milk that came to $80! In 1996! I said "hell no" and told them to take it back. I got dressed and walked down to the corner store and bought a jug of milk and a big box of Frosted Flakes for like $10. (espn.com, uncredited, "Kobe Bryant talks MJ, LeBron & *Django*, undated.)

Playing for fans

When people watch me play, I want them to see a player who's giving his all. Pouring his heart and soul onto the floor. Whether you're a Laker fan or not, like me or not, you appreciate how much passion I put toward the game. (tulsaworld.com, Bill Haisten, " 'Amazing' Kobe in OKC," February 5, 2006.)

Postponing retirement decision

I knew what I was going to do, so why wait? I'm not going to hold [Lakers'] management hostage either, because they need to start thinking about what it is they want to do [after I'm gone]. And going through this entire season not knowing, that's not fair. So if you know, let the world know and let them know. (bleacherreport.com, Tim Daniels, "Kobe Bryant Discusses Decision to Announce Retirement Early in Season," quoting from Baxter Holmes' (ESPN) interview with Kobe Bryant. February 13, 2016.)

Pushing fellow teammates

You can't afford to placate people. You can't afford to do that. You're a leader. You're not here to be a social butterfly. You're here to get them to the promised land. A lot of people shy away from that because a lot of people want to be liked by everybody. I want to be liked too. But I know that years from now they'll appreciate how I pushed them to get us to that end result. ... So when players look in the distance and see us winning championships and see us celebrating and having a good time, they think, "Oh, this is what leadership is, this is how you win, everyone gets along, we're all buddy-buddy, we all hang out, blah, blah." (si.com, 'Twilight the Saga," Chris Ballard, not dated.)

Reading

By reading, by paying attention in class and in practice, by working, I strengthened my focus. By doing all of that, I strengthened my ability to be present and not have a wandering mind. (*The Mamba Mentality: How I Play*, by Kobe Bryant, 2018.)

Recovering from injuries

There's a contingent of people that say, "Father Time is undefeated. You won't be able to do it. Blah blah blah." So part of me is saying, "Well, I know where *your* threshold is. So if this had happened to you, you'd probably quit, right?" That's the thing that I think people don't understand when they talk about Father Time, and they look at my injuries. They're equating that to others who have come before me. (The *New Yorker*, Ben McGrath, "The Fourth Quarter," March 24, 2014.)

Respecting fans' dedication

One night we had a big storm. It was raining and the bus was leaving our hotel to come here to the game and there's still people outside with Kobe signs and posters. No ponchos. Just chasing after the bus and screaming. And that's when my teammates realized it's pretty different. ... I was always popular here, but this summer in particular has been something that I can't explain." (palmbeachpost.com, Hal Habib, "Habib: Kobe Bryant, a 2 a.m. interview and a lesson in humility I'll never forget," January 26, 2020.)

Retirement

I don't know what you want to do when you retire. You're going to go through a state of depression. You're going to have an identity crisis. These are all things that were said to me because people were genuinely concerned. (*USA Today*, January 23, 2020, Mark Medina, "Life after basketball: Kobe Bryant's transition to Oscar, Emmy winner and AAU coach.")

Sacrifice

I wasn't willing to sacrifice my game, but I also wasn't willing to sacrifice my family time. So I decided to sacrifice sleep, and that was that. (*The Mamba Mentality: How I Play*, by Kobe Bryant, 2018.)

Second act

I swear, growing up as a kid, I dreamt of winning championships and worked really hard. But then to have something like this come out of left field—I heard a lot of people tell me, "What are you going to do when you retire?" I want to be a writer and a storyteller. I got a lot of, "That's cute." I got that a lot. (theatlantic.com, Jemele Hill, "The Kobe I Knew Became a Champion for Others," January 27, 2020.)

Shaquille O'Neal

We're talking every day ... We're giving advice to one another, we're pumping each other up at the same time. He's like my older brother. *Shaq played for the Los Angeles Lakers from 1996 to 2004.* (stltoday.com, footage from November 1996, filmed from KCAL, interviewed by "Chick" Hearn.)

Sneakers

You'd be surprised how little time we spend talking on

sneakers. We talk about nature. We talk about the sense of self. We talk about humanity and culture. We talk about all of these things—inspirations. And then it all inevitably comes back to the product. We believe there's a spirituality that exists in the world that connects to the product. It may sound very geeky or whatever, but that's just how we are. (*On the art of designing athletic sneakers.* Solecollector.com, Gerald Flores, "The Tao of Kobe Bryant," April 13, 2016.)

Still photography as a teaching tool

I can watch and analyze and critique. Still photos, you can learn a lot more than you can from moving pictures. Things move so fast. With a still image you actually have time to look in the moment, and look at what was working for the offensive player or not or what was working for the defensive player or not. (reddit.com, photographer Andrew D. Bernstein interview with Kobe Bryant, who has photographed him since his initial entry into the NBA, posted January 26, 2020.)

Storytelling

What I love is storytelling. I love the idea of creative content, whether it's mythology or animation, written or film, that can inspire people and give them something tangible they can use in their own lives. (SI.com, "Kobe Bryant, Through the Years," SI.com Staff, January 26, 2020.)

Surrendering

The moment you give up is the moment you let someone else win. (goalcast.com, Flavia Medrut, "25 Kobe Bryant Quotes to Help You Overcome Every Challenge," December 28, 2018.)

Success

When you make a choice and say, "Come hell or high water, I am going to be this," then you should not be surprised when you are that. It should not be something that is intoxicating or out of character because you have seen this moment for so long that ... when that moment comes, of course it is here because it has been here the whole time, because it has been [in your mind] the whole time. (inc. com, Marcel Schwantes, "15 Kobe Bryant Quotes From His Legendary Career That Will Inspire You," January 26, 2020.)

Shooting star

I've shot too much from the time I was 8 years old. But "too much" is a matter of perspective. Some people thought Mozart had too many notes in his compositions. Let me put it this way: I entertain people who say I shoot too much. I find it very interesting. Going back to Mozart [movie, *Amadeus*, 1984], he responded to critics by saying there were neither too many notes or too few. There were as many as necessary. (GQ interview in 2015, quoted by Steve Gardner, in usatoday.com, January 26, 2020.)

Stardom

It's crazy. If you sit back and start thinking about it, maybe you could be overwhelmed by the situation. You've just got to keep going slowly and keep working hard on your basketball skills. Then, I don't think your head can swell because you won't have time to think about it. (latimes.com, quoting Helene Elliott in "Column: A look back at when Kobe Bryant humbly began his leap to the pros," October 15, 1996.)

Taking a pass

You've got a lot of people paying their hard-earned money to watch you perform. It's your job to be in shape. It's your job to perform at that level every single night. And as a competitor, I'm not duckin' shit. Like, it's not "Oh, my back hurts. I'm sore. We gotta play Vince Carter and the Toronto Raptors tonight." .. So I would be in the layup line like, "Okay, there are a lot of days when you can rest and recover. Today ain't one of them. He's gonna have to see me today." (clutchpoints.com, Kenny Honaker, "Kobe Bryant goes on rant against load management," August 30, 2019.)

Teaching excellence to kids

We try to teach the kids what excellence looks like. Right? And it's not that—some of them may want to play in the WNBA, some of them may not—but we try to give them a foundation for the amount of work and preparation that it takes to be excellent in whatever it is that you chose to do. So, we're here playing basketball. We're going to focus on the details. We're going to learn the basics, we're going to learn the fundamentals. We're going to do those things over and over. And hopefully it's something that they can apply to other areas in their life."(The *Hollywood Reporter*, January 26, 2020, Evan Real, "Watch Kobe Bryant Praise Daughter Gianna, an Aspiring Basketball Star, in 2018 Interview [Jimmy Kimmel].")

Team player

I'll do whatever it takes to win games, whether it's sitting on a bench waving a towel, handing a cup of water to a teammate, or hitting the game-winning shot. (inc.

com, Marcel Schwantes, "15 Kobe Bryant Quotes From His Legendary Career That Will Inspire You," January 26, 2020.)

Telling stories

If we're able to create stories that are true, create stories that come from in to out, versus out to in. If we're chasing things that are popular or we're doing things because we believe them to be successful, then we're going about it the wrong way. We can stay true to ourselves and all of us write stories that come from within, then that is the definition of success, right? If it moves you as a writer, an author, and saying this is helping me deal with an issue that I've kind of pushed to the back, it's helped me navigate through that. If it helped me find an inner truth, then that is success. Because if that's inner truth to you, it will inevitably be a truth to somebody else. (theundefeated.com, Kelley L. Carter, "Kobe Bryant was preparing to dominate Hollywood as he did NBA," January 27, 2020.)

Tiger Woods

Tiger inspires me. But if you ask him, I bet he tells you that he doesn't feel pressure. I know I don't. [Woods] started playing golf at about the same age I started playing basketball. It's like breathing to us. It's cool. Every day, the fans want to see Tiger blow out the field at Augusta, or see me score 81 points. (tulsaworld.com, Bill Haisten, "Bill Haisten: Reflecting on two interview experiences with the great Kobe Bryant," January 26, 2020.)

Time passages

Know this above all else....Fully use every point, moment, and hour that you have. Time waits for no man... Seize the day. (esquire.com, Mike Sager, November 2007 profile, "Kobe Bryant Doesn't Want Your Love," reprinted January 2020.)

Vanessa Bryant as his inspiration

And it's about family. It's about my wife, Vanessa. You guys don't know this, but my last game that we had here against the Utah Jazz, I was really tired. I got home, and I was like, "I don't know if I can do this thing. I got one more game left, but I don't have any legs," and she said, "I want to show you something. I got a gift for you for your last game." And she proceeded to show me the row of retired jerseys from Baylor, from Magic, from Shaq, from Cap, all with personal messages signed to me, including from Michael Jordan, including from the great Bill Russell, including from the great Larry Byrd. When I saw that, I knew then that I had to turn it up ... So, thank you, baby, for being an inspiration to me." (etonline.com, "Kobe Bryant's Family Joins Him for Numbers Retirement Ceremony With the Los Angeles Lakers," December 18, 2017.)

What's left behind after retiring

I don't think I will leave anything behind, apart from the reputation of my 20-year career. I will leave the shell of who I have been for the last 20 years but what carries on is the spirit to understand how to deal with failure, handle success and communicate. These are the things that I will carry with me forever. (independent.co.uk, Tim Rich, "Kobe Bryant interview: Los Angeles Lakers legend on plans for life after basketball.")

Wizenard Book Series

Sports/fantasy is a blend of two of my passions: sports and fantasy storytelling. I'm a voracious reader and huge Harry Potter fan. So, it was a natural fit for me from that perspective. And, I think kids respond to lessons they learn while being entertained. It connects back to my desire to want to bring joy back to youth sports, while teaching important life lessons. Fantasy and magic draw people in—especially kids. And in sports, the magic is inherently there—good and bad. If I'm feeling great, if I feel like: I can't miss! That basket looks massive! But then conversely, if I'm feeling bad, the basket looks like it's the size of a keyhole. I can't make anything. That's emotional magic. So I wanted to take emotion and use that as magic in our world to teach these very complicated methods to our children in an entertaining way. (barnesandnoble.com, Rachel Sarah, "An Interview with Kobe Bryant of *The Wizenard Series*: From NBA Superstar to Author," June 18, 2019.)

Work ethic

I have "like minds." You know, I've been fortunate to play in Los Angeles, where there are a lot of people like me. Actors. Musicians. Businessmen. Obsessives. People who feel God put them on earth to do whatever it is that they do. Now, do we have time to build great relationships? Do we have time to build great friendships? No. Do we have time to socialize and to hang out aimlessly? No. Do we want to do that? No. We want to work. I enjoy working. (GQ profile, 2015, quoted by Hannah Frishberg, "Kobe Bryant's best quotes about life," January 27, 2020.)

Chapter 3

QUOTES ABOUT KOBE BRYANT

NBA Commissioner Adam Silver

For 20 seasons, Kobe showed us what is possible when remarkable talent blends with an absolute devotion to winning. He was one of the most extraordinary players in the history of our game with accomplishments that are legendary: five NBA championships, an NBA MVP award, 18 NBA All-Star selections, and two Olympic gold medals. But he will be remembered most for inspiring people around the world to pick up a basketball and compete to the very best of their ability. He was generous with the wisdom he acquired and saw it as his mission to share it with future generations of players, taking special delight in passing down his love of the game to Gianna. (nba.com, Adam Silver, "NBA Commissioner Adam Silver's Statement on Passing of Kobe Bryant," January 26, 2020.)

Sports Columnist Jason Gay

Kobe Bryant personified the modern sport alpha. On the court, he was *the alpha*, really—for better, and sometimes, worse, in greatness and defeat, demanding to put the whole game on his shoulders when it mattered most, and even when it didn't matter....Bryant played to win, period, and over his 20 seasons as a Los Angeles Laker, he won all the time, finishing with five championship rings, and a firm space among the very best to ever play the game. (*Wall Street Journal*, Jason Gay, "What Kobe Bryant

Meant," January 27, 2020.)

Sports Blog Writer Will Leitch

Since retiring from the NBA, Kobe had laid down a framework for an athlete's post-retirement life that was as groundbreaking a template as his Hall of Fame on-court career was for active players. He founded and ran a company, Kobe Inc., that worked in sports branding and ended up earning him more than $200 million when Coca-Cola bought one of the companies he'd invested in. He started a venture capital firm. He hosted his own streaming television show for ESPN. He partnered with a multi-sport training academy for young athletes.... He published a number of books. An outreach program in China made him the most popular player in the country still, five years after he left the game. He retained one of the best-selling shoe brands for Nike. *He won a freaking Oscar.* (*New York Intelligencer*, Will Leitch, "Kobe Bryant Was Just Getting Started," January 26, 2020.)

Former NBA coach Byron Scott

I tell a story a lot about Kobe at 18 years old. I would always have to come to practice early to get my treatment and get ready for practice being the elder statesman. I came in one time, and we were still playing at the Fabulous Forum, and I heard the ball bouncing. No lights were on. Practice was at about 11, it was probably about 9, 9:30. And I go out to the court and I look, and there's Kobe Bryant. He's out there shooting in the dark. And I stood there for probably about ten seconds, and I said, "This kid is gonna be great" ... I knew this kid was gonna be special. (*Byron Scott played for the Los Angeles Lakers from 1996-1997. He coached the*

Lakers from 2014 to 2016.) (*Business Insider,* Scott Davis, "Former NBA coach Byron Scott reveals the first moment he knew an 18-year-old Kobe Bryant was going to take over the league," December 18, 2017.)

His Favorite Teacher, Jeanne Mastriano

He was remarkably disciplined in high school. He was getting pulled out to play with this team or that team, and he'd be gone for days, and he'd come back with the assignments in hand. That was super. I respected him a lot for that....He would always write about basketball. He'd always talk about being a pro ballplayer. (wbur.org/onlyagame, Jeanne Mastriano, "Meet Kobe Bryant's 'Muse': His High School English Teacher, December 12, 2015.)

L.A. Sparks head coach, and former LA Laker (1996 to 2014), Derek Fisher

Kobe showed me that limits upon performance exist only in our minds. He made me realize that if you have the will to achieve something, and you put in the time and energy, it will happen....That's what makes Kobe different. He comes from the old-school with a brand of mental and physical toughness that was much more common in players before the game became more of an entertainment product. In that sense, he's one of the last basketball purists. For him, it's all about passion, competition, and ultimately, winning—not the branding, the numbers, the analytics, and everything else that has turned the game into a business commodity. (*The Cauldron,* Derek Fisher, "Without Kobe Bryant, There Is No Derek Fisher," April 13, 2016.)

General Manager for Indianapolis Colts (NFL), Chris Ballard

It's 1996, and the Lakers call in Bryant, fresh off his senior prom — he took pop singer Brandy, you might recall — for a pre-draft workout at the Inglewood High gym. In attendance are General Manager Jerry West and two members of L.A.'s media relations staff, John Black and Raymond Ridder. Bryant is to play one-on-one against Michael Cooper, the former Lakers guard and one of the premier defenders in NBA history. Cooper is 40 years old but still in great shape, wiry and long and stronger than the teenaged Bryant. The game is not even close. "It was like Cooper was mesmerized by him," says Ridder.... After 10 minutes West stands up. "That's it, I've seen enough," Ridder remembers West saying. "He's better than anyone we've got on the team right now. Let's go."(*Sports Illustrated*, Chris Ballard, "Kobe's Well-Honed Killer Instinct," May 27, 2008.)

Former U.S. President Barack Obama

Kobe was a legend on the court and just getting started in what would have been just as meaningful a second act. To lose Gianna is even more heartbreaking to us as parents. Michelle and I send love and prayers to Vanessa and the entire Bryant family on an unthinkable day.

(Twitter, @BarackObama, January 26, 2020.)

Writer Stephen King

Kobe gone? No, no, no, no, no.
No.
(Twitter, @StephenKing, January 26, 2020)

Former New York Yankee shortshop, Derek "Captain Clutch" Jeter

All I ever needed to know about Kobe Bryant was this: that throughout our friendship, the most meaningful conversations we had—they were always about family. Put aside one of the all-time great basketball careers for a second. Put aside his famous work ethic, the Mamba mentality, that incredible will to win. I'll let everyone else tackle that. ... He cared much more about being a husband to Vanessa and a dad to his girls. He loved his family—he *was* his family. That's what was important. (theplayerstribune. com, "Kobe," January 26, 2020.)

TV Talk Show Host Stephen Colbert

I feel a strange connection to [Kobe's] family and his friends and those who loved him and those who've gone through this particular tragedy—including not only the family and friends of Kobe Bryant and Gianna Bryant, but also the family of John Altabelli, Keri Altabelli, Alyssa Altabelli, Sarah Chester, Payton Chester, Christina Mauser and Ara Zobayan—because I lost my father and two of my brothers when I was a boy to a plane crash that was also in heavy fog. One of the terrible things about that shock and the heartbreaking unreality, nightmare quality of someone huge in your life who just disappears, the center of your love disappearing in that moment, is not knowing what happened.... Unlike a plane, helicopters don't have black boxes and when a helicopter goes down we don't necessarily know why it did....When a helicopter goes down, we don't know how to improve the helicopter, we don't know how to improve the flying of the pilots so this won't happen again in the future. And I hope that while nothing will possibly improve this tragedy, while nothing will take away this heartache and this pain from this family that will be living with it for the rest of their lives ... that perhaps someone could take action to make sure that there are some ways to record what is happening in these helicopters, so that it doesn't happen as often. So I hope the NTSB will do something to improve the conditions for the helicopter pilots and the information they can get when tragedies like this happen because these people are in misery. Why confound their misery with the mystery about what happened to their loved ones? It's better to know than not to know because if we know, we could possibly stop this from happening to someone else in the future. And personally, I want to send my love and my prayers to Kobe's family and all these families and know that there is something on the other side of grief. (Stephen Colbert, *The Late Show with Stephen Colbert*, January 29, 2020.)

Nike

Along with millions of athletes and fans throughout the world, we are devastated by today's tragic news. We extend our deepest sympathies to those closest to Kobe, especially his family and friends.

He was one of the greatest athletes of his generation and has had an immeasurable impact on the world of sport and the community of basketball.

He was a beloved member of the Nike family. We will miss him greatly.

Mamba Forever.

— official Nike website (nike.com)

Michael Jordan: Charlotte Hornets (NBA) owner, and Former Chicago Bulls player for 14 seasons

I am in shock over the tragic news of Kobe's and Gianna's passing. Words can't describe the pain I'm feeling. I loved Kobe—he was like a little brother to me. We used to talk often, and I will miss those conversations very much. He was a fierce competitor, one of the greats of the game and a creative force. Kobe was also an amazing dad who loved his family deeply—and took great pride in his daughter's love for the game of basketball. Yvette joins me in sending my deepest condolences to Vanessa, the Lakers organization and basketball fans around the world. (@ esteep, "Statement from Michael Jordan on the Passing of Kobe Bryant," January 26, 2020.)

Earvin "Magic" Johnson: Former president of basketball operations for the Los Angeles Lakers, for whom he played for 13 seasons

I thought he was going to live forever. I thought he was invincible. He played like that. He walked like that. He was a confident young man. We will always remember what Kobe Bryant did on the court. We will remember what he did off the court and for the city. I do not think right now that we can put it into words what he meant for Los Angeles. I will miss him. When you put on that uniform, the Laker uniform, there was nobody who took more pride in being a Laker than Kobe. It was amazing. We need Kobe to be around. And our kids who idolized him. And the fan base who idolized him. There was more for him to do. He died way too early. And he left quite a legacy. He was special. God created the special basketball player and the special man. We will miss him. He impacted the world. And very few athletes get to impact the world like Kobe Bryant did.

We used to talk about being a father and a husband. Things that were special to the two of us. I will miss the conversations that we had. We say goodbye to a hero, to a legend, to an icon. And the guy we will always love and remember in our hearts. (Phone call with CBS Los Angeles, CBS News, Chevaz Clarke, "I thought he was going to live forever": Magic Johnson pays tribute to Kobe Bryant, January 27, 2020.)

Shaquille (Shaq) O'Neal, former player for Orlando Magic, Los Angeles Lakers (1996-2004), Miami Heat, Phoenix Suns, Cleveland Cavaliers, and the Boston Celtics

I'm not doing well. I'm sick. I haven't eaten. I haven't slept. I'm looking at all the tapes. I'm sick right now. We still are the best duo ever created. That's not going to change, but I wish at 60 and 70, in the old folks' home or on a show, we could talk about it. But he will be remembered. And everyone's going to honor him and everything, but for me this is going to hurt for a long time.

I know some idiot's going to bring up the relationship me and Kobe had. Our relationship was that of brothers. All this stuff that is documented between us, it was never a dislike. It's just ... listen, this is what brothers do. I have a younger brother, we fight all the time but guess what? I love him. And I love Kobe Bryant. I'm the first to say "hey, I got four [NBA championship] rings and I know

I couldn't have gotten three without him." (cnn.com, The Big Podcast with Shaq, PodcastOne, January 2020.)

Caron Butler, former player for multiple NBA teams

He wrote Tuff Juice, *which had a foreword by Kobe Bryant*: When I first came into the NBA, I never shared my story with anybody. But when Kobe came to my house and saw me around my environment, I think he saw a lot more of the other side of my life and how I approached the way I played. I was always prompt with practice. I never quit on drills or anything like that. Life after basketball, he's a friend that I have for life. We are forever connected. For him to support me and be someone I could always call a friend, that is special. (dailynews.com, Mark Medina, "Sacramento's Caron Butler calls his friendship with Kobe Bryant 'Special,'" August 28, 2017.)

Kareem Abdul-Jabbar: former player for the Milwaukee Bucks, and the Los Angeles Lakers

It's very difficult for me to put in words how I feel about the loss of Kobe Bryant. As a young boy, I met him when he was 11, 12 years old. I was friends with his dad, Joe. We were former adversaries; Joe played for the 76ers, but he was a good friend and someone that I shared a friendship [with]. And it's hard for me to understand now how this is affecting Joe and his wife. So to Kobe's family I want to send my most sincere and heartfelt regrets and prayers. My thoughts are with you guys.

Kobe was an incredible family man. He loved his wife and daughters. He was an incredible athlete and a leader in a lot of ways. He inspired a whole generation of young athletes. He was one of the first ones to leave high school, come into the NBA and do so well, dominating the game and becoming one of the best scorers that the Los Angeles Lakers has ever seen.

I had the privilege of being there when he scored his 81-point game, and it's something I will always remember as one of the highlights of the things that I have learned and observed in sports. Kobe, my thoughts are with you absolutely. Rest in peace, young man. This loss, it's just hard to comprehend. Go with God. (nypost.com, Justin Tasch, "Kareem Abdul-Jabbar posts poignant tribute to Kobe Bryant," January 27, 2020.)

LeBron James, LA Lakers player

I'm not Ready but here I go. Man I sitting here trying to write something for this post but every time I try I begin crying again just thinking about you, niece Gigi and the friendship/bond/brotherhood we had! I literally just heard your voice Sunday morning before I left Philly to head back to LA. Didn't think for one bit in a million years that would be the last conversation we'd have. WTF! I'm heartbroken and devastated my brother!! Man I love you big bro. My heart goes to Vanessa and the kids. I promise you'll continue your legacy man! You mean so much to us all here especially #LakerNation and it's my responsibility to put this shit on my back and keep it going!! Please give me the strength from the heavens above and watch over me! I got US here! There's so much more I want to say but just can't right now because I can't get through it! Until we meet again my brother!! #Mamba4Life #Gigi4Life (Posted by LeBron James on his Instagram page, quoted in bleacherreport.com by Scott Polacek, "LeBron James on Kobe Bryant's Death: 'I Promise You'll Continue Your Legacy.'")

Chapter 4

BY THE NUMBERS

A Top NBA Scorer: 32,683 points.

Highest Single-Game Point Scorer: 81 points, in a game against the Toronto Raptors, on January 22, 2006.

Jersey numbers: 8 and 24 (both retired): As Kobe explained, "When I first came in at 8, [was] really trying to 'plant your flag' sort of thing. I got to prove that I belong here in this league. I've got to prove that I'm one of the best in the league. You're going after them. It's nonstop energy and aggressiveness and stuff. ... "...Then 24 is a growth from that. Physical attributes aren't there the way they used to be, but the maturity level is greater. Marriage, kids. Start having a broader perspective being one of the older guys on the team now, as opposed to being the youngest. Things evolve." (cbssports.com, "Why Kobe Bryant changed jersey numbers and what No. 8 and No. 24 meant to the NBA Legend," Shanna McCarriston, January 27, 2020.)

Longevity: 20 years playing for the NBA (highest in the league)

Height: 6 feet, 6 inches.
Weight: 212 pounds.
Age: 41 years old.
From basketball-reference.com:
1,346 games

25 points
5.2 total rebounds
4.7 assists
44.7% - field goal percentage
32.9% - 3 point field goal percentage
83.7% - free throw percentage
48.2% - effective free throw percentage
172 – Win Shares

$1,015,000 – starting salary for the 1966-97 NBA season (LA Lakers)

$25,000,000 – ending salary for the 2015-2016 NBA season (LA Lakers)

Career highlights:
• five-time NBA champion
• 11-time first-team selection
• 2008 MVP
• 2-time Finals MVP
• 18-time All-Star
• 4-time All Star MVP
• Gold medal, USA Basketball, Beijing Olympics (2008)
• Gold medal, USA Basketball, London Olympics (2012)

Chapter 5

KOBE BRYANT CHRONOLOGY, PERSONAL AND PROFESSIONAL

1978

Kobe Bean Bryant is born August 23, 1978 in Philadelphia, Pennsylvania to former NBA player Joe Bryant and Pamela Cox Bryant.

1984

The family moves to Rieti, Italy so his father can play professional basketball, having retired from the NBA.

1991

The Bryant family returns to the U.S., settling in Ardmore, Pennsylvania.

1992

He attends Lower Merion High School. As a freshman, he plays on the varsity basketball team.

1996

He's named Southeastern Pennsylvania's all-time leading scorer: 2,883 points, surpassing Wilt Chamberlain.
He's named Naismith Prep Player of the Year while playing the position of shooting guard for Lower Merion High School in Ardmore, Pennsylvania.

He's named *USA Today* High School Boys' Basketball

Player of the Year.

He's named Gatorade High School Basketball Player of the Year.

He's named First-Team *Parade* All-American.

He's the 13th draft pick for the Charlotte Hornets, who immediately trade him to the Los Angeles Lakers. He signs a three-year rookie contract for $3.5 million.

1997

He wins the Slam Dunk Contest, the youngest champion ever at age 18.

He's named to the NBA All-Rookie Second Team.

1998

He's the runner-up for the NBA's Sixth Man of the Year Award.
He's named starter for the NBA All-Star team and scores a team-high 18 points for the Western Conference.

2000

Los Angeles Lakers win their first championship since 1988, beating the Sacramento Kings.

NBA All-Star team.

NBA All Defensive First Team.

2001

NBA Championship: Lakers beat the Philadelphia 76ers.

McDonald's signs him to a $10 million endorsement deal.

Nike signs him to a $40 million endorsement deal.

He marries Vanessa Laine.

2002

NBA Championship: Lakers beat the New Jersey Nets.

NBA All-Star game MVP.

2003

NBA All-Defensive First Team.
All NBA First Team.
NBA All-Star.

Their first daughter, Natalia, is born on January 19.

2004

Lakers lose NBA Championship to the Detroit Pistons.

All-NBA First Team.

NBA All-Defensive First Team.

NBA All-Star.

2005

NBA All-Star.

He scores 62 points in three quarters against the Dallas Mavericks. He outscores the Mavericks team 62-61, the only time a player has done this through three quarters since the introduction of the shot clock.

2006

NBA All-Star.

All NBA First Team.

NBA Season Scoring Champion.

Their second daughter, Gianna, is born on May 1.

2007

NBA All-Star Game MVP.

NBA Season Scoring Champion.

Gold Medal, FIBA Americas Championship.

2008

NBA Most Valuable Player.

NBA All-Star.

All NBA First Team.

Gold Medal, Summer Olympic Games. ("The Redeem

Team" defeats Spain, 118-107.)

2009

NBA All-Star Game MVP.

All NBA First Team.

All NBA Defensive First Team.

NBA Championship: Lakers beat the Orlando Magic.

NBA Finals MVP.

2010

NBA All-Star.

All-NBA First Team.

NBA All-Defensive First Team.

NBA Championship: Lakers beat the Phoenix Suns.

NBA Finals MVP.

2011

NBA All-Star.

NBA All-Star Game MVP.

All-NBA First Team.

NBA All-Defensive First Team.

2012

NBA All-Star.

All-NBA First Team.

Gold Medal, Summer Olympic Games.

2013

NBA All-Star.

All-NBA First Team.

Forbes lists him the fifth highest paid sports star in the world.

He co-founds the venture capital firm, Bryant Stibel, to provide strategy, capital, and operational support to businesses with a focus across technology, media, and data.

He founds Kobe Inc., to take more direct control of his business affairs. The company's first investment is a 10% stake in sports drink Body Armor.

2014

NBA All-Star.

2015

NBA All-Star.

He tears a rotator cuff in his right shoulder and undergoes season-ending surgery.

He announces that he will retire at the end of the 2015-16 season.

2016

He scores an NBA season-high 60 points in his last game. *Forbes* lists him as #33 on the list of America's richest entrepreneurs under 40; his net worth listed as $350 million.

He founds the multi-media content company, Granity Studios, with the goal of "creating new ways to tell stories around sports."

Their third daughter, Bianka, is born on December 5.

2018

He wins a Sports Emmy Award for Outstanding Post-Produced Graphic Design for his animated short film, *Dear Basketball*.

He wins an Annie Award for short subject.

He wins the Academy Award for Best Animated Short Film, *Dear Basketball*.

He publishes a nonfiction book, *The Mamba Mentality: How I Play*.

2019

Their fourth daughter, Capri, is born on June 20.

In December, he is nominated as an inductee to the Naismith Memorial Basketball Hall of Fame.

2020

January 26: He, his daughter Gianna, and seven others died in a helicopter crash in Calabasas, California.

January 31: A short memorial service is held for Kobe and Gianna Bryant, and the others in the helicopter crash.
February 24: A public memorial service is held, "A Celebration of Life: Kobe & Gianna Bryant."

August: Kobe Bryant will be posthumously inducted in the Naismith Memorial Basketball Hall of Fame (Springfield, Massachusetts).

Chapter 6

TAKEAWAYS

There are recurring themes in Kobe's life, lessons learned, the road taken, and not taken, all of which gives us much food for thought as we contemplate how best to live our own lives. A wise man, it is said, learns not only from his experience but also from the experience of others: life's too short to learn everything on your own. Fortunately, by studying the other lives of people, taking those to heart, we too can learn from those who went before, those who inspire us, and those who raise us up with them. That was Kobe's enduring challenge.

We Are Family

More than anything else, Kobe Bryant was a family man, and he always stressed the importance of family, which kept him grounded. A doting father and loving husband, he explained that he *loved* basketball, but he loved his family even more. So when he retired, he spent time with his family instead of going to Lakers games to relive the past, to bask in the glow of public approbation; he focused on his family, and his extended family—young athletes at his own training facility, Mamba Sports Academy (Thousand Oaks, California). Family? First, last, and always.

Work Ethic

Kobe's work ethic is legendary. He pushed himself up to, and beyond, his physical and mental limits, and he pushed his teammates just as hard. Hard work, he knew, gave him a cutting edge—just work harder than anyone else. No breaks. Go the extra mile. Just do it.

Matt Given (inc.com, "This 1 Quote From Kobe Bryant Is All You Need to Know About His Success," subtitled "One of the all-time NBA greats' work ethic will amaze you," December 19, 2017), explained that "Bryant would show up for 7 a.m. practices at 5 a.m. After high school practices, he'd make teammates stay to play games of one-on-one to 100. Lakers head coach Byron Scott would find a sweaty 18-year-old rookie Bryant in a darkened gym, two hours before practice, doing individual shooting and dribbling drills. He routinely outworked the NBA's best players. During the run-up to the 2008 Olympics, he did full predawn workouts before official practices started."

No Pain, No Gain

Time and again, Kobe worked through the pain on the basketball court. As he's explained in interviews, there are other players who want to take the night off after an injury, or when they were not feeling up to the game—a perspective Kobe never embraced. Like every other player on the court, he had his fair share of pain, but unlike them, he pushed on, grimacing through the pain, to get the job done—to score, to win the game. It's pushing beyond your physical limits, not because you want to but because you *have* to. Nobody pushed his own body as hard as Kobe did. *Nobody*.

The Power of Passion

From the beginning, Kobe fell in love with the game of basketball, and it showed. In "Dear Basketball," a poem he wrote, he limned his unquenchable passion for everything about the game. "Dear Basketball," he wrote, "I fell in love with you." It was a love that lasted a lifetime, going back to when he was 6 years old, until the day he died at 41.

Likewise, when he retired from basketball, to the surprise of those that didn't know him, he turned to a lifelong passion, storytelling, because he wanted to inspire children, the next generation. He felt that the future belonged to them, and his job was to prepare them for that future, so they too could realize their potential to the fullest.

He credited his high school English teacher for instilling and igniting that passion in him. "She was so good and passionate about what she was teaching about writing and storytelling. She firmly believed that storytelling could change the world. And she opened my eyes to this passion I didn't know existed." (usatoday.com, "How Kobe Bryant's forgotten homework assignment sparked his post-NBA career," Mark Medina, January 23, 2020.)

Time on Your Side

No one was more aware of the transient nature of time than Kobe. He didn't waste time—he utilized it efficiently and effectively. Time is a precious and irreplaceable resource, and must be treated as such. Kobe did. Time, he knew, was fleeting. He knew how easy it was to fritter time away, hang out with friends, kick back, relax, watch TV, but he also knew those weren't the best uses of his personal time. Family, first of all, and then self-improvement in every way. If he had a motto, this would be it: No Time to Spare.

Paying Attention to Detail

The devil's in the details, and to conquer the devil, it

meant having a granular approach to everything, to deconstruct it to its basic building blocks, to work from the foundation on up, like a building contractor. He took nothing for granted, and assumed nothing. He scrutinized everything with microscopic intensity, and by the time he was finished, he knew what he wanted to know. There'd be no surprises. Whether it was a play on the basketball court, a business deal, a marketing plan, or products that bore his name, he made sure he did his homework because it always pays off in the end.

Always a Student

Kobe was a lifelong student. Sitting in the locker room with his swollen feet in a tub of iced water, he took the time to read: not recreationally but vocationally. His mind was like a sponge wanting to soak up as much information as possible. He'd be on a plane, headed to his next game, and instead of taking a nap or thumbing through a flight magazine, he'd watch videos to deconstruct his own moves on court, and that of others. He had an insatiable appetite for knowledge, on and off court. Never complacent, never thinking that he was at the top of his game and didn't need to learn anything else, he took a granular approach to studying everything he could, on any subject that interested him, because he wanted to *know*.

Giving It More Than Your Best Shot

Mike Sager shares an anecdote that underscores the dedication and focus of Kobe Bryant. In early 1999, after breaking a finger bone that handicapped his ability to make free throws, Kobe decided to take matters in his own hands. "To correct the flaw, he said, he went to the gym over the summer and made 100,000 shots. That's 100,000 shots *made*, not taken. He doesn't practice taking shots, he explained. He practices *making* them. That always stuck with me. They talk a lot in basketball about 'doing things the right way.' Kobe loved basketball so he took no short cuts. He knew there was nobody to cheat but himself. The next season, 2000, the Kobe/Shaq Lakers won their first of three NBA championships." (esquire.com, "The Summer Kobe Bryant Made 100,000 Shots," November 30, 2015).

Follow Your Bliss

Reading is not a national pastime, and in the NBA, it's not likely that a lot of the players find recreational reading, especially storytelling as found in novels, to be a principal interest. But for Kobe, storytelling was *everything*. He knew the power of words, the power of storytelling, the importance of telling the age-old stories of good versus evil, of inspiring dreams, of framing stories in ways that children could understand, and learn from, them. He *knew*. So, after his retirement from basketball, he started a company to issue book-length fiction, movies, and other media with the purpose of hooking young readers with entertaining storylines, so that he could inspire them.

Few people know that among his favorite possessions were signed copies of J.K. Rowling's first Harry Potter novel (*Harry Potter and the Sorcerer's Stone*), and George R.R. Martin's epic saga ("Fire and Ice," known to HBO viewers as *Game of Thrones*). They didn't know what a voracious reader he was, and that he read, and loved, fantasist J.R.R. Tolkien's epic story, *The Lord of the Rings*, in which a war for the One Ring, a ring of power that would give its wearer dominion over all of Middle-earth, was taken by—of all people—a small hobbit named Frodo Baggins who assumed the weight of the world, which hung in the balance. He said, quietly, "I will take the ring, though I do not know the way."

Kobe was a man who unapologetically read fantasy, whereas businessmen prefer biographies of famous sports figures or business moguls, and nonnutricious Wonder bread books like *Who Stole My Cheese?* He loved books, and most of all, storytelling, which he wanted to pass on to his four daughters, because he wanted them to be, like him, lifelong readers. He knew that developing a passion for reading had its own joy, and its own rewards.

Chapter 7

More About Kobe Bryant

First and foremost, every fan should have Kobe's own book, *The Mamba Mentality: How I Play*, with photos by Andrew D. Bernstein. Speaking in his own voice, explaining how he approaches the art and craft of playing basketball, Kobe's passion for the sport is inspirational. Indispensable reading for fans. The 208-page book, published in 2018, costs $35.

Dear Basketball (written, narrated by Kobe Bryant; directed, animated by Glen Keane; music by John Williams. Running time, 5 minutes. 2017.) This won an Oscar at the 90th Academy Awards in the category of Best Animated Short Film. A poignant poem set to music and cartoons, it encapsulates Kobe's life in a way you won't ever forget.

Granity Studios (granitystudios.com), Kobe Bryant's multimedia company launched in 2016, publishing original content with a sports-oriented focus with engaging stories to educate and inspire young readers.

Kobe's definitive biography has yet to be written. In the interim, however, I recommend *Kobe Bryant: The Inspiring Story of One of Basketball's Greatest Shooting Guards*, by Clayton Geoffreys, who has written an extensive series of books on basketball players, including Michael Jordan, LeBron James, Shaquille O'Neal, and others. Written principally for children and young adults (age level 8 to 18), this book is an eminently readable overview of Kobe's life and career. Published in 2014, the book, unfortunately, is outdated but still worth your time. $9.99.

For a look at the nuts and bolts of playing basketball, *Facing Kobe Bryant*, edited by Sean Deveney, is fascinating reading—especially for newcomers to the game. Subtitled "Players, Coaches, and Broadcasters Recall the Greatest Basketball Player of His Generation," the 176-page book is filled with unique perspectives that can only be gleaned by those intimately involved in the game. $14.99.

For an overview to Kobe's career from an authoritative publisher, you can't go wrong with a one-shot by Sports Illustrated: *Kobe, Special Retirement Issue: From Kid to Champ to Leader to Legend, Two Decades of Photos and Stories from SI.* Available from Amazon.com as a print-on-demand publication, this 104-page, full color overview of his basketball career belongs in the collection of every fan—especially young adults who will love the numerous photos. $15.99.

Kobe: The Storied Career of a Lakers Icon, from the staff of the *Los Angeles Times*, is an oversized (9 x 12 inch) hardback book of 304 pages. This is a coffee table book drawing on two decades of reportage from the local newspaper. A must-have for any fan. (Note: Available exclusively from the latimes.com store, they won't ship it overseas.) $59.95. There will be more video documentaries about Kobe in the years to come, but in the interim fans should see *Kobe Bryant's Muse* (Showtime, 1 hour, 23 minutes, 2015), available for streaming from Amazon.com for $9.99.

For sports memorabilia, buy direct from the source, from established brands, like Nike.com. (Caveat emptor: When a celebrity like Kobe Bryant dies, scammers set up fake websites to sell bogus, or non-existent, goods; crooks put up fake goods online auction sites, *especially* signed products like jerseys, basketballs, and books; and some scammers set up fake websites to capture your credit card information. Be careful! Deal only with reputable sellers, and not the crooks that raise their piggish snouts from the mud to sniff a quick buck at your expense.)

Kobe on social media (as of January 29, 2020)
- Facebook.com/Kobe (21 million followers)
- Twitter.com/kobebryant (15 million followers)
- Instagram.com/kobebryant (19 million followers)

Chapter 8

RATTLING THUNDER

We like to think that the story of our lives is like a novel or a movie, with everything wrapped up in a neat, pretty bow, because that's comforting. But that's not necessarily the reality of life. On that fateful day, January 26, 2020, Kobe Bryant and eight others boarded a Sikorsky helicopter and lifted off at 9:06 a.m. from the Santa Ana-John Wayne airport. The others included 13-year-old daughter Gianna, a budding basketball talent; head coach of the Orange Coast College Pirates, John Altobelli, his wife Keri, and their youngest daughter, Alyssa; Sarah Chester, and her 13-year-old daughter, Payton; Christina Mauser, a defensive specialist for Kobe's club team, the Mambas; and pilot Ara Zobayan, Kobe's private pilot.

They were headed to a youth basketball tournament at Kobe's Mamba Sports Academy in Thousand Oaks, California. They never arrived. Flying below cloud cover, in foggy weather, the twin-engine Sikorsky S-76B slammed into a hillside in what the National Transportatioin Safety Board termed "a high-energy impact crash" in Calabasas, California.

There were no survivors.

We live, unfortunately, in a media-driven society in which the rush to be the first to announce news eclipses the need to be accurate. Move fast and break things. So it was no surprise that, even before the victims' families could be

oid news site, TMZ, broke the tragic news,
h insufficient consideration to the surviving
ers whose lives had permanently upended,
rmoil, overcome by unfathomable grief. But
ot alone. As Margaret Sullivan pointed out
in the *Washington Post* ("In Kobe coverage, bits of grace
amid chaos," January 28, 2020): "But what rules the media
world in 2020 is the drive to be first, at any cost, and the
rush to get something—*anything*, it sometimes seems—on
an outlet's site."

The media pile-on included President Donald Trump,
who hastily tweeted wrong information about the number
of fatalities, along with others who went off half-cocked,
significantly the British Broadcasting Company (BBC),
known for its staid news organization. All of this repre-
hensible behavior was more than merely a public embar-
rassment—it was a media disgrace.

As is always the case, the agonizing details emerged
piecemeal, too slowly for a stunned world hungering for
any morsel of verified information; many held out hope
that somehow, miraculously, there'd be survivors, that
God's grace would touch Kobe and the others, that somehow He would give us a miracle to save the day.

But there were no miracles that day—only stone-cold
reality, which set in early. The fact, simply, was this: Kobe
Bean Bryant was gone. Only 41 years old, Kobe had so
much to live for, so much to give, so much to be shared. He
and the others on that ill-fated helicopter ride were far too
young to die such untimely deaths. Each person a candle
burning bright, suddenly snuffed out, reminding us of one
of the hardest lessons of all: Against the randomness of the
universe, nothing can protect us.

Awash in grief, thousands of stunned fans in southern California, many wearing sports jerseys bearing number 24 in his honor, flocked to the Staples Center in downtown Los Angeles, the venue where Kobe Bryant made basketball history. Others flocked to the crash site, to Calabasas, California, because they wanted to see where the helicopter, laden with 800 pounds of fuel, slammed into a hillside, igniting a conflagration that scorched the earth.

Kobe Bryant had dreams that will go unfulfilled. After two decades as a professional basketball player, he smoothly shifted gears in retirement to helm his own media company, because he loved the art of storytelling, instilled in him long ago by an English teacher, Jeanne Mastriano.

Kobe anticipated his retirement in 2016 with a poem titled "Dear Basketball" that encapsulated his relationship to the game in a handful of lines. "I fell in love with you," he wrote. It was a love that never abated.

In the poem he acknowledged it was his time to leave the game. "I'm ready to let you go," he wrote, because after decades of walking into basketball arenas to do battle, he had given his all, and his mortal body took the unremitting abuse—the punishing body blows, the unforgiving slams, the pushing and the shoving, and painfully falling on the unforgiving hardwood floors. It was time to retire, he knew, and move on with no regrets.

The poem was the basis of an animated short film written and narrated by Kobe, with animation by Glen Keane, and music by John Williams. "Dear Basketball," which ran only five minutes, earned him a Sports Emmy Award for Outstanding Post-Produced Graphic Design, an Annie Award for Best Animated Short Subject, and an Academy Award for Best Animated Short Film.

Those who didn't know of Kobe's burning desire to be a storyteller after he retired from basketball were surprised that among his business deals, he started his own media company, Granity Studios (granitystudios.com). As its website states, "...Granity Studios is an award winning multimedia original content company focused on creating new ways to tell stories about sports. Stories that are crafted to entertain, by bringing education and inspiration together. We partner with award-winning writers, producers and illustrators to awaken the imagination of young athletes and foster emotional and mental development that allows them to reach their full potential."

When Kobe first came on the scene, straight from high school and into the NBA, comparisons to Michael Jordan were inevitable. But from the beginning, though Kobe was quick to acknowledge "Air" Jordan's dominance, he didn't want to have a reputation based on being the heir apparent. Kobe learned from Jordan, who became a mentor and lifelong friend, just as he learned from the other greats in the basketball field—a number of them showing up at the Staples Center at Kobe's retirement ceremony. Kobe didn't want to be *like* Mike. He wanted to be himself; he then encouraged those who followed, like LeBron James, to go even further, to carry the ball to new heights.

The last tweet that Kobe posted, the day before he died, was on LeBron James's Twitter account. Kobe wrote to congratulate LeBron on become the third-highest scorer in the NBA, eclipsing his own record, just behind Kareem Abdul-Jabbar and Karl Malone. LeBron has accumulated 33,644 points (January 2020). Kobe wrote to congratulate

Kobe Bean Bryant, with his own wings, soared high to kiss the sky.

Chapter 9: Fadeaway

"Mamba Out"

by Kobe Bryant

Man, guys, I can't believe how fast twenty years went by. This is crazy. This is absolutely crazy. And to be standing here in center court with you guys, my teammates behind me, and appreciating the journey that we've been on. We've been through our ups and we've been through our downs, and I think the most important part is that we all stayed together throughout.

I grew up a die-hard, I mean a die-hard Laker fan, die-hard. I knew everything about every player that has played here. So to be drafted and then traded to this organization and to spend 20 years here, I mean, you can't write something better than this.

I'm more proud, more proud of the fact that not about the championships, but about the down years, because we didn't run. We played through all that stuff, we got our championships, and we did it the right way. And all I can do here is just thank you guys, thank you guys for all the years of support, thank you guys for all the motivation, thank you for the inspiration.

What's funny, the thing that had me cracking up all night long was that I go through twenty years of everybody screaming to pass the ball and on the last night they're like "don't pass it!" [he laughs]

This has been, this has been absolutely beautiful. I can't

believe it comes to an end. You guys will always be in my heart, and I sincerely, sincerely appreciate it. No words can describe how I feel about you guys. Thank you, thank you from the bottom of my heart. I love you guys, I love you guys.

My family, to my family, my wife Vanessa, my daughters Natalia and Gianna, thank you guys for all your sacrifice. For all the hours I spend in the gym working and training, and Vanessa, you holding down the family the way that you have, I can't, there's no way I can thank you enough for that. So from the bottom of my heart, I thank you.

What can I say? Mamba out.

— facebook.com, ESPN, "Kobe Bryant Farewell Speech – 'Mamba Out,'" transcribed and edited by Luke Ellison, January 28, 2020.

Vanessa Bryant

You can walk away knowing you've always played with everything you have, babe. I'm so proud of you. I'm proud of everything you've given to all your fans even [when] you weren't feeling your best. You've always pushed through it because you played for those fans that sacrificed so much to see you play in person. You mean so much to us all. I'm so excited to see what God has in store for us as a family now that one chapter is closing and new ones are opening. We love you! (Instagram posting, reprinted in hellomagazine.com, "Vanessa Bryant pays sweet tribute to husband Kobe on his retirement," November 30, 2015.)

Chapter 10

In Memoriam

In addition to Kobe Bryant and his daughter, Gianna, seven other people lost their lives. The hometown newspaper in Los Angeles, in stark contrast to many other news sources, took the time to explain a little about who the other passengers were on the helicopter involved in the fatal crash.

From the **Altobelli** family: **John** (father), **Keri** (wife), and **Alyssa** (daughter).

John was a baseball coach for Orange Coast College for 27 years, winning 700 victories. **Alyssa** was a teammate of Gianna Bryant. Alyssa played point guard at Kobe Bryant's Mamba Sports Academy.

Christina Mauser: the top assistant coach of the Mamba Academy girls' basketball team.

Ara Zobayan: Bryant's private helicopter pilot who flew the Sikorsky for Island Express Holding Corp. He was a seasoned flier with two decades of experience in the cockpit.

From the Chester family: Sarah (mother) and **Payton** (daughter).

Payton was a student at St. Margaret's Episcopal School in San Juan Capistrano. She played basketball with Gianna Bryant at Mamba Sports Academy.

In Vanessa Bryant's Instagram posting on January 29, 2020 to her 6.5 million followers, she urged fans to support the MambaOnThree.org. The donations go to help the Altobelli, Mauser, Zobayan, and Chester families, who would be most grateful for any support.

Instead of buying a pair of sneakers, a jersey, or other memorabilia to remember him by, open your heart—and your wallet—to make a difference in their lives with a timely, and distinctively felt, and much appreciated donation.

The other charity worth your money is the Mamba and Mambacita Sports Foundation, named after Kobe and Gianna. Its web address is: mambamambacitasports.org.

⚜

Vanessa Bryant's Instagram Post

My girls and I want to thank the millions of people who've shown support and love during this horrific time. Thank you for all the prayers. We definitely need them. We are completely devastated by the sudden loss of my adoring husband, Kobe—the amazing father of our children; and my beautiful, sweet Gianna—a loving, thoughtful, and wonderful daughter, and amazing sister to Natalia, Bianka, and Capri.

We are also devastated for the families who lost their loved ones on Sunday, and we share in their grief intimately.

There aren't enough words to describe our pain right now. I take comfort in knowing that Kobe and Gigi both knew that they were so deeply loved. We were so incredibly blessed to have them in our lives. I wish they were here with us forever. They were our beautiful blessings taken from us too soon.

I'm not sure what our lives hold beyond today, and it's impossible to imagine life without them. But we wake up each day, trying to keep pushing because Kobe, and our baby girl, Gigi, are shining on us to light the way. Our love for them is endless—and that's to say, immeasurable. I just wish I could hug them, kiss them and bless them. Have them here with us, forever.

Thank you for sharing your joy, your grief and your support with us. We ask that you grant us the respect and privacy we will need to navigate this new reality.

To honor our Team Mamba family, the Mamba Sports Foundation has set up the MambaOnThree Fund to help support the other families affected by this tragedy. To donate, please go to *MambaOnThree.org*.

To further Kobe and Gianna's legacy in youth sports, please visit *MambaSportsFoundation.org*.

Thank you so much for lifting us up in your prayers, and for loving Kobe, Gigi, Natalia, Bianka, Capri and me. #Mamba #Mambacita #GirlsDad #DaddysGirls #Family

– posted on Instagram, January 28, 2020

Donate to:

- MambaOnThree.org
- MambaSportsFoundation.org
- mambasportsacademy.com/mamba-mambacita-sports-foundation

Mamba Sports Academy issued the following statement on the tragic events of Jan. 26, 2020:

The Mamba Sports Academy family is devastated by the passing of Kobe Bryant, his daughter Gianna, and the seven other people lost on Sunday. We send our love and thoughts to the Bryant family and to the families and friends of Alyssa, John, and Keri Altobelli; Payton and Sarah Chester; Christina Mauser; and Ara Zobayan.

Kobe Bryant was so much more than a partner in Mamba Sports Academy. He was a caring father, husband, coach, and champion of youth sports. We mourn not only one of the greatest athletes of all time, but an active and engaged member of our community, and a visionary whose impact was only beginning to be felt by society. He will be remembered most for the care he placed and pleasure he took in educating the next generation, none more so than Gianna, Alyssa, Payton and their Mamba teammates.

Through the shared values of attention to detail, relentless pursuit of passions, and dedication to excellence, we remain committed to honoring Kobe's mission of inspiring the next generation of leaders in the world of sports and beyond.

CODA:

JANUARY 31, 2020,
A NIGHT TO REMEMBER

Kobe was a force of nature, deep and obsessed with excellence. He was wise, determined, passionate. A visionary beyond measure. A dedicated and loving husband, and a "girl-dad" like no other. When he walked into a room, the energy ignited. He was high voltage, with a motor that had no limits. His mind had an infinite capability to learn. He was, simply put, the most inspirational athlete of our time. What the world may not know, is that he was also the best friend anyone could ever imagine.

— *Rob Pelinka, Lakers General Manager, excerpted from a longer eulogy, January 30, 2020*

❊

Pregame

It was a night to remember at the sports arena formally named the Staples Center but informally known as the House that Kobe built, in downtown Los Angeles, where it's not unusual for basketball games to go into overtime.

This time, however, it wasn't another basketball game, but the game of life: a time to remember, and memorialize, the loss of one basketball's legendary players. Thousands of people united in their collective grief—mostly local fans, basketball players from the home team and the Portland Trail Blazers, the management of the LA Lakers, the media, and others. The event was the first game after Kobe Bryant's death. All 20,000 seats in the bleachers of the sports center occupied, each seatback draped with a distinctive yellow garment—a sight to see, a veritable sea of Kobe t-shirts. On the front side, Kobe's last name and the number 24, and a stylized logo (KB); on the back, his last name, the number 8, and the logo. High in the rafters, behind the last row of seats, Kobe's retired jerseys side by side: Number 8 on the left, Number 24 to its right.

Courtside, two shirts that stood out from all the rest, marked with bouquets of red roses on the seats. Draped over the two folding chairs: a black shirt with the number 2 emblazoned on the front, sporting the distinctive Nike "swish" symbol, with the word "Mamba" printed, memorializing Kobe Bryant's basketball-playing daughter, Gianna; and to its right, a Lakers shirt with the number 24, memorializing her father. In life, and now death, on a heart-breaking day, they both shared a symbolic presence on the court, their seats flanked by more fold-up chairs with the t-shirts given to the fans.

Outside, the "Fan Zone" was a shrine to Kobe Bryant. Fans worldwide came to pay their respects with a plenitude of gifts, on display until February 3, when they were to be collected and, at the request of Vanessa Bryant, boxed to be sent to her. As Lee Zeidman, president of the Staples Center, explained, "Vanessa had reached out to us and said,

'Our family would like the items out there.' So we're going to catalog every one of them. By that I mean, t-shirts, letters, basketballs, stuffed animals, toys. We're going to put those in specially made containers and we're going to ship them to the family," (*LA Times*, Broderick Turner, January 31, 2020). He noted, by that time, the fan memorial "...will have been a week. We have contractually obligated events that are moving in." In other words, it would time to move on.

The gifts included mostly flowers, which will be mulched and used as compost for the surrounding grounds. The artifacts included candles in glass, pictures of Kobe, posters, wreaths, basketballs, shoes, jerseys, and baseball caps. But it was the personalized items—sneakers, basketballs, jerseys, and white boards—with heartfelt inscriptions that made one's eyes sting with tears upon reading them: "You were my first jersey ... You made #LA Lakers the way they are today ... Mamba, keep coaching your princess in heaven ... thank you for teaching all of us the Mamba Mentality. I wouldn't have played the game without your influence. Mamba Forever. ... You taught me to strive for greatness and to never be satisfied. You are the reason I played basketball and the vital reason of why my brother and I are close. I am heartbroken. I miss you already. Your legacy will live on. LA loves you. Laker 4 life (Bryan C.)" One inscription, in neatly printed text, was written in an Asian language, which seemed so appropriate because Los Angeles is a town that is known for, and celebrates, its diversity.

The inscriptions adorned the sidewalk and grounds, including a life-size white poster board covered with handwritten farewells in felt tip pens, a board taller than those who wrote on it, and wider than it is tall.

The displayed items from the LA Lakers were, appropriately, full color images of Kobe Bryant, the largest being an action photo of him soaring through the air, eyes fixed on the basketball rim, a second or two away from slam dunking the ball.

Fans who wanted entry into the game that night, accustomed to $200 for a ticket, were not surprised that tickets for this particular game would soar due to high demand and scarcity. According to wtkr.com, a radio station in Los Angeles, the tickets two days before the game sported asking prices soaring over a thousand dollars, and at least one pair of courtside tickets offered at a record sum—$47,000 or more—any takers? The radio station noted that the ticket prices for the Lakers' subsequent game, against the San Antonio Spurs, reverted to normalcy, $200.

Like the fans, the players paid their pregame respects, in their own way. The home team wore Kobe Bryant jerseys during the warmups, each player marking this special night, one suffused with poignancy; they felt their hearts breaking, as they mourned the loss of one of their fallen comrades. It was an unforgettable night.

Before the game began, the memorial service paid homage to Kobe. The Lakers basketball team was overcome with emotion. There may be no crying in baseball, but there certainly was in basketball that night: Grown men wept unashamedly—towering giants, all of them over six feet, muscled, athletes in their prime, tough guys who played a rough game, manly men. But they all shared a communal pain, and they made no apologies for their open displays of love for a teammate whose long, muscular arms once embraced them on and off the court, in times of celebration and sorrow.

The memorial service began with a musical rendition of "Amazing Grace" by Usher, hitting all the right emotional notes.[1] Concurrently, the massive, circular Jumbotron played a six-minute video predominated with clips of Kobe being interviewed; the background music played was "Hallelujah," Leonard Cohen's classic.

"Straight to the heart."

Although it was Kobe's night, all eyes were on the heir apparent, a comrade in arms and close family friend, LeBron James, who, with tears in his eyes, spoke after Usher sang. Knowing he would be asked to say a few well-chosen words approved by the Lakers management, he prepared a written statement, but he didn't read it. He stood there, overcome with emotion, and simply dropped the paper on the hardwood floor—letting go, just as he'd had to let go his "brother" Kobe. Instead, LeBron opened up his heart to everyone, spoke plainly, and touched everyone who was present with his words.

The *Los Angeles Times* provided a transcript (January 31, 2020) which I'm quoting in its entirety, because every word should be counted.

Footnote 1• It wasn't lost to those at the sports arena that Usher's name was suffused with symbolism. If you were to look that day on Google's home page, its company logo was artfully rendered with an unmistakable tribute to Kobe and Gianna: The letter G, and to its right, two different colored seats, representing Kobe's and Gianna's at the sports stadium, and the remaining letters in its name. Google's dictionary has three definitions of *usher*, all resonant with meaning: "a person who shows people to their seats, especially in a theater or at a wedding," "an assistant teacher," "show or guide (someone) somewhere," and "cause or mark the start of something new." All of them apply in this instance regarding Kobe Bryant and the others who perished with him.

LeBron James Speaks from the Heart

Before I get started with this speech that I have, I want to acknowledge all the lives that were lost Sunday morning. Alyssa Altobelli. John Altobelli. Keri Altobelli. Payton Chester. Sarah Chester. Christina Mauser. Ara Zobayan. Gianna Bryant and Kobe Bryant.

Now, I've got something written down. They asked me to stay on course or whatever the case may be, but Laker nation, I would be selling y'all short if I read off this shit. I'm going to go straight from the heart.

The first thing that came to mind, man, is all about family. As I look around this arena, we're all grieving. We're all hurt. We're all heartbroken. But when we're going through things like this, the best thing you can do is lean on the shoulders of your family. And from Sunday morning all the way to this point — and I've heard about Laker Nation before I got here last year, about how much of a family it is — and that's absolutely what I've seen this whole week. Not only from the players, not only from the coaching staff, not only from the organization, but from everybody. Everybody that's here, this is really, truly, truly a family. And I know Kobe, Gianna, Vanessa and everybody thank you guys from the bottom of their hearts as Kobe said. Now I know at some point, we will have a memorial for Kobe. But I look at this, I look at this as a celebration tonight. This is a celebration of the 20 years of the blood, the sweat, the tears, the broken-down body, the getting up, the sitting down, the everything. The countless hours, the determination to be as great as he could be. Tonight, we celebrate the kid that came here at 18 years of age, retired at 38 and became probably the best dad we've seen over the past three years, man.

Before we get to play [enthusiastic yelling from fans]. Love ya'll, man. Kobe's a brother to me. From the time I was in high school, watching him from afar to getting in this league at 18, watching him up close. All the battles we had throughout my career. The one thing that we always shared was that determination to just always want to win and just want to be great. The fact that I'm here now means so much to me. I want to continue along with my teammates, to continue his legacy, not only for this year, but for as long as we can play the game of basketball that we love because that's what Kobe Bryant would want.

So in the words of Kobe Bryant, 'Mamba out.' But in the words of us, 'Not forgotten.' Live on, brother.

❦

After that, everyone observed 24.2 seconds of silence for Bryant and the others who died in the helicopter crash, followed by the singing of the national anthem, by Boyz II Men.

As the LA Times reported, "After [they] sang the national anthem, a tearful LeBron James turned toward Anthony Davis and they both held each other. Davis' eyes were still red when he came through pregame introductions, and Kobe was introduced by public-address announcer Lawrence Tanter, along with the other starters: "Number 24, 6-6, 20th year from Lower Merion High School, *Kobeeee* Bryant."

The halftime show was highlighted by Khalifa and Charlie Puth singing "See You Again." There wasn't a dry eye in the crowd that numbered 20,000 fans who were touched. When they finished, Khalifa said quietly, "To the late Kobe Bryant. Peace and blessing to his entire family. His legacy is gonna be remembered. We love you, Kobe."

❀

That evening's takeaway wasn't that the Los Angeles Lakers lost to the Portland Trail Blazers (127-119), which is a minor footnote in the games for that season, and in the grand scheme of things as life goes; the takeaway is that Kobe Bryant and the others will never, ever be forgotten.

A Celebration of Life:
Kobe & Gianna Bryant

2.24.20
STAPLES Center
10 AM

Because demand for tickets to their public memorial service far exceeded supply, a lottery was held to insure that everyone had an equal chance to get a ticket at face price: 20,000 tickets were available, but 80,000 were requested. All proceeds for the tickets, which ranged in price from $24.02 to $224—numbers tied to Kobe and Giana's jerseys—went to a family charity named after them, the Mamba and Mambacita Sports Foundation.

Twenty thousand family, friends, and fans marked their calendars for February 24, 2020, a date for the memorial that resonated with meaning: 2 represented the jersey number for Gianna; 24 represented the jersey number for Kobe; and 20 represented the two decades that Kobe played for the Lakers.

The event, titled "A Celebration of Life: Kobe & Gianna Bryant," bore a single graphic: butterflies in flight, a deliberately symbolic image. Butterflies, on average, live only a month. The image symbolized the fleeting nature of life itself—in this case, Kobe and Gianna's, whose lives were cut short by a tragic accident, along with the others on that ill-fated helicopter flight.

Given that only a fourth of the fans who wanted tickets were able to get them, and concerned about tens of thousands of fans showing up on that date to show their final respects, the word went out that if you didn't have a ticket, *do not show up*. For that reason, the stadium's outdoor screens were turned off: If you had a ticket, you were one of the lucky ones; and if you didn't, you'd be able to see it online, courtesy of the Lakers management team.

At 10:30 a.m., the memorial service began with music by Beyoncé, who sang two songs—"XO" and "Halo." The songs were accompanied with quick clips of Kobe playing basketball. The lighting was appropriately colored blue, symbolizing the somber mood of the event itself.

Following the singer, the voice of an announcer said that late-night talk show host Jimmy Kimmel would "guide you through" the celebration of life for Kobe and Gianna. Visibly touched, Kimmel's voice cracked as he explained, "Everywhere you go, you see his face, his number..." During his introduction, the camera panned the audience, focusing principally on basketball players, all impeccably dressed in tailored suits, who came to pay their last respects to one of their own.

As it turned out, the line-up of hand-picked speakers covered the gamut of Kobe's life, personal and professional: It would begin with his widow, Vanessa Bryant, followed by Diana Taurasi (WNBA star), Sabrina Ionescu (basketball star, University of Oregon), Rob Pelinka (GM, Lakers), Michael Jordan (Chicago Bulls), and Shaquille O'Neal (teammate, Lakers). All carried prepared texts to the podium, because they knew that without a blueprint, they'd simply lose it, awash in grief. It was, they knew, no time to wing it.

Forever and Always

Kobe's wife Vanessa, appropriately, shed light on Kobe and Gianna from a personal, not professional, perspective. She opened her heart, sharing moments with her late husband and daughter who, as she pointed out, were inseparable. She began by talking about their 13-year-old daughter, with an anecdote about how Gianna (Gigi) would always kiss her before heading off to school, but had forgotten to do so on one day. So Vanessa texted Gigi to ask why, and the girl replied that she *did* kiss her. As Gigi explained, when she saw her mother sleeping, and didn't want to awaken her, she kissed her and then quietly left.

Vanessa's "baby girl," as she called her, took some of her notable traits from her father. Gigi loved sports, but most of all she loved basketball; Gigi also spoke Mandarin and Spanish. She was, as her mother pointed out, very smart. "She was always herself," Vanessa said, voice breaking. "I miss her so much."

"I won't be able to tell her how gorgeous she looks on her wedding day. I'll never get to see my baby girl walk down the aisle, have a father-daughter dance with her daddy, dance with me on the dance floor, or have babies of her own … Gigi would likely have become the best player in the WNBA. She would have made a huge difference in women's basketball. … I love you so much, Gigi, I miss you every day. I love you…"

Then she spoke about her husband, "My soulmate. He was my sweet husband, and the beautiful father of our children. He was my everything. He was the most amazing husband. I was fire, he was ice. He was thoughtful, even while working hard. He gifted me the actual notebook and the blue dress in *The Notebook* movie. When I asked him why, he said it was the scene where Allie comes back to Noah. We had hoped to grow old together, like the movie. We really had an amazing love story."

"I want my daughters to know and remember the amazing person, husband, and father he was, the kind of man who wanted to teach the future generations to be better and keep them from making his own mistakes."

When she finished, there was not a dry eye in the stadium. She spoke simply, plainly, and from the heart, and touched everyone.

Sabrina Ionescu

Standing over six feet tall, Sabrina Ionescu, a senior at the University of Oregon, plays for the Oregon Ducks. Though eligible for the WNBA when she turned 21, she elected to stay in school, to finish up her senior year and graduate, after which she may elect to step up to the pro league.

Citing Kobe as an inspiration ("I grew up watching [him]. I wanted to be just like him."), she admired and emulated his relentless work ethic. Her daily routine: "Wake up, grind, and get better."

When she came to know Kobe, she found not only a mentor but a friend, and paid it forward to mentoring his daughter, Gigi, who confided in her that when she grew up, she wanted to play college ball as a Huskie for the University of Connecticut. (Beyond that, Gigi had clearly set her sights on the WNBA.)

Sabrina explained that even though she knew Kobe was gone, she still sent him texts, though there would be no response. "Sometimes I find myself still waiting," looking for a sign. Then one day, as she watched a yellow-colored sun set with a helicopter crossing the sky, she got the sign she had been waiting for. It was an emotional moment for her, a symbolic one, as she realized that for both Kobe and Gianna the sun had finally set.

Luigi "Geno" Auriemma

Following Sabrina, who explained Gianna's desire to be a college ball player as a Huskie for UConn, its head coach, Luigi Auriemma, took the ball she passed and went for an emotional slam dunk. Luigi, now 66, was painfully aware of the transient nature of time, as he contrasted his own life with that of Gianna and her generation by noting, "This is always about the children. We've lived our lives, we have a little bit left, and they're just starting their lives."

He focused on the importance of "dad-ness," of being there for the children, and spoke of his conversations with Kobe, who coached the team his daughter played on—Team Mamba—and how he pushed them, albeit gently, toward being the best they could be.

Rob Palinka

The general manager for the LA Lakers, Rob knew Kobe for 20 years, during the time he played for the team—an unbroken record for longevity in the league. Rob's carefully chosen words gave an overview of his relationship with Kobe—his best friend, a father, and a husband. In a copy of Kobe's first fantasy novel, *The Wizenard Series: The Training Camp*, Kobe inscribed a copy to him: "To RP, my brother. May you always remember to enjoy the road, especially when it's a hard one. Love, Kobe."

He shared anecdotes, ending with one that showed how much Kobe loved his wife, showering her with thoughtful gifts, including mastering Beethoven's "Moonlight Sonata," which he learned how to play just for her. It was, Rob noted, a difficult piece to master, but without any prior training, and learning by ear alone, Kobe's gift for memorizing came into play, hitting all the right notes on the piano's keys and also emotional notes in his wife's heart.

Michael Jordan

Much has been written about the relationship between Kobe and Michael, who at first were adversaries, then friends, and finally brothers. With tears running down his face, Michael cried unashamedly, exposing his big heart. He considered Kobe to be his little brother who, like other younger brothers, was a pain in the butt, but grew up to be an essential part of his life. Calling him up long past midnight, Kobe wanted to learn from the best; he would call Michael and pepper him with questions about the fine art of playing basketball: post-up moves, footwork, and, of course, the triangle offense to counter the defensive tactic dubbed the [Michael] Jordan Rules. "He left it all on the floor," Michael said, tears running down his face. Sharing more anecdotes that shed light on Kobe's unquenchable desire to be better, to always seek self-improvement, Michael noted, "He wanted to be the best basketball player that he could be."

One in particular stood out: On a visit to Los Angeles, to see his former coach, Phil Jackson, then the coach for the Lakers, Michael showed up in a business suit, as he always does when traveling. Kobe saw him and asked, "Did you bring your shoes?" Michael replied, "No, I wasn't thinking about playing."

Kobe, you see, *always* thought about playing. Though the trip was for Michael only a social visit, it was for Kobe an opportunity to go one-on-one with one of his mentors, a basketball legend who gave no quarter on the court—just like his Kobe.

Michael shared another anecdote about their mutual passion for basketball: In one texting conversation, Kobe asked Michael about what he was doing when he was twelve years old. "I was trying to play baseball." Kobe, who assumed that Michael was driven to play basketball at an early age like him, texted him back: "Laughing my ass off."

But basketball, of course, was no laughing matter for Kobe, who had found his lifelong passion as a child—to play basketball, the subject of his Oscar-winning short animated film, "Dear Basketball." As Michael explained, talking about himself and Kobe, his "attitude to compete and play against someone he felt could enhance and improve his game ... [is] what I loved about the kid. No matter where he saw me, I was a challenge, and I admired him because of his passion. You rarely see someone who's looking and trying to improve each and every day, not only in sports but as a parent and a husband. Kobe never left anything on the court. And I think that's what he would want us to do. No one knows how much time we have. That's why we must live in the moment, to enjoy each and every one we come in contact with. Please rest in peace, little brother."

Michael's heartfelt tribute brought down the house. He got a standing ovation, and loud, sustained applause.

Shaquille O'Neal

Much has been said about Kobe's personal and professional relationship with his teammate Shaq, with whom he played for eight years. It was at times a contentious relationship borne of Kobe's desire to bring out the best in every player, including Shaq. Kobe's directness and honesty with Shaq was pure Kobe, but Shaq, like a firmly planted mountain, stood his ground—all seven feet of him. As Shaq explained, "Kobe and I had a very complex relationship over the years." But at the end of the day, off the court, when the cameras were turned off and the fans went away, Kobe would turn to Shaq and say, "Let's go whip some ass."

No matter how much the fans debate whether Shaq was right or Kobe was wrong, or vice versa, a salient fact remains: The Lakers' "three-peat" (coined by Phil Jackson) would not have been possible if the two hadn't been on the same team, figuratively and literally, and they knew it, and so did everyone else—the Lakers management, the team members, the fans, and the press at large. Basketball, as Kobe drilled into the other players, was a *team* effort, and he made sure everyone knew that. It was all about teamwork and winning.

Like Michael Jordan, Shaq got a standing ovation and sustained applause. Both giants in the field, towering over their peers, they both paid tribute to their friend, their brother, a comrade on the court.

"Mamba Out"

It was appropriate that the ceremony ended with Kobe on the court one last time, dressed in a tailored suit, and not his beloved jersey, number 24. He spoke at his retirement ceremony of the great players that came before him—a citation of the basketball greats—and shared a private moment that showed how much his wife loved him, and how those basketball greats loved and respected him: Before his retirement, she had contacted all of her husband's friends whom he admired or had played with—a line-up of the very best players in the league, past and present. Each had signed their own jerseys, inscribing them with heartfelt sentiments, paying homage to him.

More than all the honors given to him over the years, the citations and awards, those jerseys meant the world to him: He had earned the respect of the very best basketball players in the world, whom he also counted as friends, and nothing on the court could mean more. Kobe knew that he was one of them, one of the best who ever played the game; and like them, he'd inspire future generations of ball players to come. That was what it was all about. It was, as Sabrina Ionescu pointed out earlier in the tribute, all about "Wake up, grind, and get better." He was, clearly, the Black Mamba on court, a ferocious competitor who strikes like lightning, attacking his prey.

Christina Aguilera

The memorial closed with Christina Aguilera singing Franz Shubert's elegiac "Ave Maria." It ended at 12:30 p.m., and immediately after the stadium was emptied, life went on: at 7:30 p.m., the Clippers would play the Memphis Grizzlies.

A Flight of Angels

Kobe and Gianna Bryant's final resting place is close to their home in Newport Beach, California. Interred on the grounds at Pacific View Memorial Park, father and daughter are together forever. "God knew they couldn't be on this Earth without each other," Vanessa Bryant had observed during the memorial service. "He had to bring them home to have them together. Babe, you take care of our Gigi, and I got Nati, BiBi and KoKo, and we're still the best team. We love and miss you, Boo-Boo and Gigi. May you both rest in peace and have fun in heaven until we meet again one day. We love you both and miss you forever and always … Mommy."

PUBLISHED BY 8+24 BOOKS
LOS ANGELES, CALIFORNIA

Second Edition
Printed in the U.S.A.

"Even when you realize that you need to appreciate the time and the moment, it still goes by so fast."

— Kobe Bryant,
NBA TV, *Kobe: The Interview,* 2015

Made in the USA
Monee, IL
26 June 2024

60691287R00056